Carved in Stone

Carved in Stone

Rodney Grosskopff

Published by Paper Bag Publishing

Distributed by Lewis Masonic
www.lewismasonic.com

ISBN 978 0 620 47080 3

First published 2010
Reprinted 2011

Managing editor: Pat Hopkins
Editor and typesetter: Louis Greenberg
Cover design: Michael Smith

Set in 11.5/14pt Goudy Old Style

Printed in England by Ian Allan Printing Ltd, Hersham, Surrey KT12 4RG.
www.ianallanprinting.co.uk

To my wife Eileen, who has fed more Masons than any other lady in the world and encouraged me to put these words down

Contents

Introduction

These are the stories of famous Freemasons who helped develop and mould the history and culture of South Africa. But it is really one saga as they were all members of the same Masonic Lodge, Lodge de Goede Hoop, in Cape Town. Each account started as a research document for presentation in various forums, mostly at Masonic functions, but here I have taken the liberty of adding creative flesh to those dusty bones. Although this is not a narrative about Freemasonry, my good friend and editor, Pat Hopkins, felt that a brief explanation of its history, practices and aims might be helpful.

There are many theories about the origins of Freemasonry, but most accept that its practices and aims were inspired by the Medieval Operative Masons. In Europe in the Middle Ages young men were unlikely to have a career path other than in the footsteps of their fathers. If older brothers had filled available posts then the village elders would place them as apprentices with someone who had no sons to avoid a concentration of youth in one occupation. The idea behind masons' organisations was to train young men as masons so that they would be able to find work elsewhere when that in their town was complete.

Stonemasons tended to move to where there were major building projects; they were among the first skilled migrants. Many of their jobs were in far-flung places, often in towns where they were greeted with suspicion and hostility from the local community. To counter this, they needed to be extra careful in their behaviour so the masons evolved their own systems of discipline, education, worship, and care for the sick, indigent and elderly. Most lodges and guilds played a part in the community and church by raising funds and making donations through such events as harvest festivals. A very popular way was to stage a mystery play, a re-enactment of a biblical story, which also served as the format for young members' lessons.

Arriving at a building site a mason would report to the Master of the Works, prove his skills and by secret handshakes and passwords would be allocated to a lodge (which has its origin in the French word for a lean-to structure, *lodgement*) if successfully concluded. The so called Masonic secrets were necessary signs of recognition because masons did not have certificates of qualification. They therefore developed codes which they called degrees to distinguish the various grades of workmen and the pay they should receive.

The lodge had its own hierarchical structure, which has largely been retained into the present. It was presided over by a master assisted by two wardens, who allocated the work, saw that it was done properly and administered discipline. Then there were administrative officers such as the secretary and treasurer as well as special officers like the almoner, who took care of the affairs of members who were hurt or killed; the director of ceremonies, assisted by an inner guard and outer guard, who kept members on the straight and narrow, presided over meetings and preserved their privacy; and deacons, who were charged with educating young masons in their craft as well as other aspects of life. For this the deacons used masonry tools and many of their lessons have entered mainstream culture in the phrases 'square deals' and 'I'll level with you', and the use of the gavel as the force of conscience.

In the first degree, sometimes called initiation, the young man was taught to be a good citizen of the world, love his neighbours, and respect those in authority as well as his trade. In the second degree, also known as the fellowcrafts degree, he was taught to appreciate all that God has created in nature and science while increasing his skills and responsibilities. In the third degree, or Master's degree, he was invited to contemplate his ultimate destiny through which he could appreciate that a good and righteous life was worth more than money or power. He was also encouraged to lead and help those below him. As Masonry spread, the orders and degrees of the brotherhood were adapted or added to.

Many lodges found themselves in remote areas without normal services like worship and funerals, so they did the best they could. This gave rise to the Masonic Funeral, which continues today in the form of a memorial service known as a Lodge of Sorrows or Lodge of Mourning.

At some time, outsiders started to associate with Masons as their eternal principles struck a chord with them. Amongst the earliest were James IV of Scotland and William St Clare, who were invited to participate in Masonic teachings and mysteries. Soon lodges sprang up without any association to operative Masons and spread throughout the world as Freemasons' organisations. In June 1717, four Masonic lodges got together in London to form an association which they called Grand Lodge to regulate Freemasons and direct their activities.

Initially there were only two degrees. These grew into the three degrees described above, once Freemasonry became 'speculative' (no longer attached to the building industry). Various organisations invented numerous degrees each with a new lesson, which many lodges simply added to their library of workings, and soon this became unmanageable. How to deal with this situation led to a schism between two opposing views of Freemasonry. The Antients believed that in a normal craft lodge they should be able to work as many of the new orders as they wanted, which is the way Masonry developed in the Cape. The Moderns, on the other hand, believed that pure and ancient Freemasonry consisted only of the three craft degrees and the Holy Royal Arch. And if they wanted to perform the other degrees they should form a new body. The thinking of the Moderns was prevalent in England, and would be exported to Holland.

At the time Freemasonry did not exist in Holland, but soon thereafter the young Duke of Lorraine, Francis Stephen, decided he wanted to be a Freemason. The Grand Lodge of England wasted no time and sent a high-level delegation to Holland to initiate him into the craft in 1731. This created a great interest in Freemasonry there and elsewhere in Europe and the first continental lodges were formed by 1734. Francis was destined for greater things and in the same year left Freemasonry in the hands of Count Vincent de la Chappelle as Grand Master. But even as he took his place in history he remained a friend to Masons and was happy to buck Rome on behalf of Freemasonry.

In the beginning, Dutch Freemasons were happy to take leadership from England and their early lodges were formed with English warrants, but following a convention on 2 March 1770, the Grand Lodge of the United Netherlands, which had been previously formed, took control of their own destiny. At the time the private Dutch East India Company (VOC), run by the Heeren XVII, was operating a refreshment station at the Cape.

While the settlement there was Dutch it had been influenced by French and Swiss mercenaries and the arrival of the French Huguenots in the late 17th century. In fact, Cape Town was often referred to as Petit Paris du Sud. The first suggestion of Freemasonry here came from Jacobus Cornelis Matthews Rademacher, a senior VOC merchant who called at the city when homeward bound from Java. On his return to Holland in 1764 he recommended that steps be taken to found a lodge, which led to the appointment of a ship's captain, Brother Abraham van der Weijde, as a roving ambassador for Freemasonry in the Company's colonies. He arrived at the Cape on 24 April 1772.

Part 1

The Start of Freemasonry
in the Cape

Chapter 1
Abraham van der Weijde

The red brick building off a little square in Amsterdam was decorated with stone corners, lintels and sills. A nondescript door opened onto an entrance hall that told an altogether different story. It was simple, but with an elegance that spelt money. The room, simply furnished with a hardwood desk and three comfortable leather chairs around a coffee table near a generous fireplace, was dominated by a huge painting covering one wall. Abraham van der Weijde did not know much about art, but it looked like a Rembrandt to him. It depicted a group of men witnessing the signing of a document. They were mostly dressed in black with white ruffs, though one or two showed a flash of colour. He recognised two faces peeping out of the darkness in the back row: Baron Carl Boetzelaer and Isaac van Teylingen.

The VOC were expecting him and he was sent to the second floor, which not many people ever visited. Van der Weijde was intrigued, intimidated and proud to be there. The stairs were lined with tall paintings – at least one was a Rembrandt and perhaps another, but there were also portraits by Pieter Paul Rubens and Frans Hals and those bearing signatures of artists he had never heard of. He was dressed much like them, in a black embroidered silk vest with silk-covered buttons, black serge trousers and high boots, with a crisp white starched ruff, all relieved by a black ostrich feather in his hat. 'Sober but elegant,' he thought. At first glance, some of the portraits even looked like him with their short pointed beards and sharp moustaches. But few would have had his vigour, or his leathery face with its slightly watery eyes from years at sea.

He had hardly sat down in the vast empty lobby when the double doors opened and van Teylingen escorted him into the boardroom of the VOC. The walls were divided by a parade of gold Ionic pilasters, which took their rhythm from the line of windows on one side. The red wall panels in-between bore giant gilt-framed portraits of past chairmen. Below them were sideboards laden with silver and crystal. There were fourteen people seated around a table made for seventeen in the room that, he realised, was the setting for the Rembrandt painting in the entrance. None were wearing ruffs and he immediately became self-conscious, but they didn't seem to notice. He was conducted to a chair next to Boetzelaer, whom he knew as an adjutant to Prince William of Orange and a member of the States General, Grand Master and member of the united Netherlands government.

'It's good of you to come,' said Boetzelaer, giving him a warm handshake. 'Just relax, you're with friends.'

'Captain van der Weijde,' said the chairman. 'You may be wondering why we have invited you here today. Well, two of the Heeren XVII are very senior Freemasons. The most worshipful Brother Baron Boetzelaer and right worshipful Brother van Teylingen are respectively the Grand Master and Deputy Grand Master of the Grand Lodge of the United Netherlands. They are also part of the Heeren XVII, who run one of the most powerful companies in the world.'

Van der Weijde was aware that the VOC was similar to a state within a state. It controlled ten times the territory of the Dutch Government and had a force of 10 000 soldiers and 100 men-of-war to go with their 150 trading ships. It was an organisation in need of civil structures.

'You may have heard of Jacobus Cornelis Matthews Rademacher,' continued the chairman as a tall, gaunt gentleman half rose and nodded. 'He recently made a tour of our possessions and has submitted a report, which he'll now briefly outline.'

Rademacher unfolded his report and in a dry, harsh voice read, 'The VOC sent Jan van Riebeeck to establish a refreshment station at the Cape of Good Hope in 1652. It soon became one of the most important stopovers on route to the East – so much so that it's now known as "The Tavern of the Seas".'

The chairman waved his hands like a conductor trying to chase Rademacher on, but he took no notice. 'As the population grew, slowly at first then faster, culture found a fertile community in which to take root. Churches, schools and theatres were established and there are balls at the Castle. So has Freemasonry taken root, but in a haphazard sort of way.

'A young German Mason named Abraham Chiron has got together a few of the older men who arrived in the Cape as Masons and they are trying to get a lodge started. We support his efforts because we need our people to have as many other interests as possible to occupy their minds. Nevertheless, we want to keep an eye on what happens, and it will require the authority of a manager of the VOC and a senior Freemason to get it on a proper footing. In this regard you're perfect.'

'What do you think?' asked Boetzelaer, putting his hand on van der Weijde's arm.

'I think I can do the job. I'd need some mandate.'

'You've just got it.'

'With respect, mynheer, I need some appointment, a rank perhaps, which would give me the authority. I fear I may be received with some resentment.'

The chairman had had enough. 'Carl, Isaac and Jacobus, work out the details with the captain.'

The four gathered down at the end of the table as the rest made their way to lunch.

Boetzelaer, who was now in charge, turned to Rademacher. 'Can you frame the authority?'

'Yes,' squirmed Rademacher.

'While I'm not impressed by titles, people in the colonies are,' added van der Weijde.

'What have you in mind?' asked van Teylingen.

'Perhaps Deputy Grand Master and Plenipotentiary?' van der Weijde muttered

'I'm Deputy Grand Master,' van Teylingen retorted.

'Then Second Deputy Grand Master and Plenipotentiary.'

'There's no such rank, we have to follow protocol,' rasped Rademacher.

'What is the protocol for this situation?' interrupted Boetzelaer. 'Let's go with Abraham's suggestion. We want you to be on the *Paauw*; it leaves for Cape Town next Friday.'

***

Captain Snyders was waiting for van der Weijde on the docks in Amsterdam when he arrived in the VOC carriage with his luggage.

After shaking hands they melted away to a pub to talk.

'What are you carrying?' asked van der Weijde.

'Bordeaux wine, Madeira and brandy; 10 000 bottles for Pondicherry in India.'

'Sounds like a good trip.'

'Not that good, we've only got a pint a day, white Nantes for the first month then Languedoc red,' sighed Snyders. 'I also have flour, salt, meat, copper, lead and sheet iron. Oh, and we have the *klomptjie* bricks in the hold as ballast. And we'll stop in Cadiz to collect some gold.'

'Who'll accompany us?'

'The *Meewtjie* and *Princess Wilhelmina*; we meet *Duc de Penthievre* and another French ship at Cadiz.'

When they got back to the ship it was still a hive of activity. The hold was already full and the 100-strong crew were lashing goods down on the deck where there was even a pen for live animals. On board van der Weijde was invited to share the captain's cabin.

The start of the voyage was a little rough as they were caught in the tail end of the contrary winds in the Gulf of Gascony. Van der Weijde was happy to spend a few days in relaxed Cadiz where the food was interesting, the wines heady and the women intoxicating. It was a welcome break from the confined space on board and the overbearing stench of humanity. It was with some reluctance he forced himself back on the *Paauw*; he was getting too old for this.

After passing the Canary Islands they took advantage of the north-westerly along the African west coast, where the *Duc de Penthievre* stopped in Senegal to pick up slaves. From there they caught the erratic winds south of the Cape Verde Islands, where it took all of Snyder's skill to navigate across the equator. Then they took a route west of the Ascension Islands, skirted Brazil and picked up the westerly to take them back towards Africa and Table Bay.

Van der Weijde had been to Cape Town many times, but never tired of its magic. He was disappointed at the first view as the fog was low on the water and he could see very little, but as the *Paauw* approached, the lion wriggled free of its fleece, first its rump then its head, and by the time they were close in, the majestic Table Mountain reared up behind Lion's Head like a wall covered with a table cloth of pure white damask. Luis Vas de Camoes's words from *Lusiadas* came flooding through his mind:

> By fleecy locks the mighty mass is crowned
> Grandeur and danger compass it around
> With front of adamant, its lengthening shape
> Presents the Guardian Genius of the Cape.

The town looked like a scattering of sugar cubes in the bowl of the mountains. Its features were too small to point out other than the foreboding fort and the hospital which dealt with sick sailors and recently had to contend with two smallpox outbreaks. This is what Sir Francis Drake had seen when he exclaimed, 'This Cape is the most stately thing, and the fairest cape we saw in the whole circumference of the earth.'

Seafarers have been awestruck by the magnificence of the mountains of the Cape Peninsula ever since Bartholomeu Diaz opened a sea route round Africa to the East in 1488. By 1772 there were over a thousand substantial houses in the bowl between mountain and sea. The streets were wide and lined with oaks and as they sailed into harbour van der Weijde could make out a few of the other major buildings.

'The town was built by van Riebeeck and his successors,' writes C. Pama in *Vintage Cape Town*. 'They started building, a new environment gradually took shape in very much the same way as medieval towns had developed in far-off Europe. First a fort for protection against known and unknown enemies, men and beast alike. Then barracks, a hospital, houses for farmers and tradesmen, boarding houses and taverns for the passing sailors, a slave-lodge for cheap labour. Finally, a handsome church, whose ancient tower became a landmark that could be seen for many miles away.'

The Castle, bristling with cannons, was by far the most imposing building. There had been fortifications before it built by the Dutch, British and Danes to protect the fresh water supply and the landing place in Table Bay. Van Riebeeck's primary orders were to establish a garden to provide passing company ships with fresh fruit and vegetables and to strengthen the town's defences. Shortly after arriving he built an earthen-walled fort near the shore in the vicinity of what is now the Grand Parade. The present fort, started in 1666, was designed by the engineer Pieter Dombaer and completed three years later.

The Castle is designed in the shape of a pentagon with bastions dedicated to the titles of the Prince of Orange at each point. It was as busy as a small town, with officers' accommodation, kitchens, pay office, the arsenal, workshops, gunsmiths; in addition, the garrison was barracked there. The bastions were connected by thick stone walls which were lined on the inside with residences, government offices, storerooms and stables. Simon van der Stel had the gateway moved to halfway between Buren and Leerdam in 1682. Planned to resemble the brick-and-stone town entrances common in Holland, it was topped by a belfry. In 1691 the internal courtyard was divided in two by a *kat*, or defensive wall. On either side were built the official quarters of the Governor and senior staff as well as a great hall, which at first was used mainly for religious services. Later an ornamental balcony known as *de nieuwe kat* was added to the facade.

For over a century the Castle was the centre of life in the settlement. People gave birth and died there. There was pomp and ceremony, glittering balls and extravagant banquets. There was also disease and despicable deeds committed in the infamous *Donker Gat* (Dark Hole) – a dank underground prison complete with torture chamber. Nearby were three frowning gallows on a small hill. Noted one visitor: 'I came to the conclusion that they were meant as a warning to arriving strangers not to outrage the laws of the country; otherwise the new arrival might meet a disgraceful death beneath these beams.'

The Grand Parade

Van der Weijde could hardly wait to get off the *Paauw* just so he could take a walk in the town. Meeting with Acting Governor van Plettenberg could wait. On disembarking he walked past the Castle, over the Parade and through the company gardens below the proud Government House to Ben Nörthling's guesthouse near the Heerengracht. There was a feather bed waiting for him with clean sheets, a bath and crisp towels. After revelling in those luxuries he dressed as best he could from his crumpled kitbag as Johanna Nörthling had taken his best suit.

First port of call was the seafront with its taverns and restaurants and he was happy to sit at a table with a first-class beer in his hand and watch the ladies go by in their tight bodices and hooped skirts. Governor Ryk Tulbach's puritan laws insisted on demure kappies, but they did not hide their flashing eyes and shy smiles. Later he found a restaurant and a table in the corner, wanting to be alone after the crush of the voyage. But Snyders, with a handsome lady on his arm who he introduced as Hester, found him and rearranged the table to accommodate them. Hester said she had a friend who was not doing anything, but van der Weijde declined the offer and left as soon as good manners would permit.

When he woke the following morning it was to find that Johanna Nörthling had done wonders with his black outfit, which now had a white collar and was clean and ironed. He dressed and headed for the breakfast room where he turned down the mielie porridge, but accepted eggs, lamb's liver soaked in milk and fried with chunks of bread hot out of the oven and drenched in butter. Coffee was set before him without being requested.

It was a pleasant day as he made his way to the Castle to introduce himself to the acting Governor, van Plettenberg, standing in for Ryk Tulbach who was too frail to perform his duties. When he got there, it was to find that word had already got round about his arrival and he was ushered into van Plettenberg's office. While the acting Governor already knew of his meeting with the Heeren XVII, he initially only wanted to speak of 'home'. It was a while before van der Weijde was able to steer the conversation to the purpose of his visit.

'Rademacher sends his regards. He remembers you well,' said van der Weijde.

'A bit of a bore, no?'

'They're all interested in the Cape. The chairman asked me to give you his personal greetings; as did Baron Boetzelaer and van Teylingen.'

'Oh, the Freemasons.'

'Yes, they hope I will be able to organise the Masons properly here.'

'I'll arrange for you to meet Christoffel Brand and young Chiron. They seem to be the ringleaders.'

'Why "ringleaders"? Do they give you trouble?'

'Not at all. The more I can find to occupy people's minds the better.'

'Perhaps you should join them, the English lords say it helps them keep control and breeds loyalty.'

'Ha! I have no time for it and I would hate to align myself with one group. Do come to dinner tonight, my wife would love to hear as much as possible about home.'

Van der Weijde was flattered and accepted without a second thought. Van Plettenberg made a practice of inviting visiting dignitaries home to the Castle for dinner so he could keep abreast of developments in Holland.

The Castle was a dreary place and the Governor's quarters only a little better. The armoury – a sort of entrance hall festooned with coats of arms and a display of halliards – was set up for drinks. There were only men present, strutting around looking to impress with their fancy but outdated finery – there was even someone with a ruff. Snyders was there, obviously without the advantage of Mrs Nörthling to straighten out his best suit. They retold the same stories of Holland over and over until mercifully they were called to the table where a few ladies were present. He found himself between the First Lady, who had put together a surprisingly good meal, and Mrs de Wet, wife of the magistrate, with van Plettenberg across from him.

'They tell me the ladies in Europe now adopt the French way and wear no hats to formal functions,' said the First Lady patting her hat, which dropped onto her shoulders more like a collar. 'The old Governor, Ryk Tulbach, left us with these ridiculous dress codes, one of which is that ladies should wear hats at all times. I suppose it makes sense with the sun in the day, but we've had to adapt it for night.'

'My dear Lady van Plettenberg, French women powder their hair white and arrange all manner of decorations in it,' replied van der Weijde. 'Somehow they pile their hair higher and higher; as much as two feet on top of their heads. Our ladies are much more restrained, a little powder here and there to suggest nobility I am told, and a piece or two for sparkle.'

He enjoyed entertaining the women, charming them about life in the major cities of Europe, but the Governor was becoming more and more exasperated as he wanted to know of more important matters.

'And what of the war between France and England, Captain van der Weijde?' he interrupted.

'Well, there's no war for the moment, but they're both itching for a fight. England is trying to keep the French out of the Americas.'

'And everywhere else for that matter, but that shouldn't affect us as we're a neutral trading company.'

'Sir, it's my personal opinion that we'll be denied the luxury of neutrality,' replied van der Weijde.

'England has always been a friend to Holland and Prince William of Orange is close to their royal family. They'll always support us.'

'They may be forced to turn against us.'

'Fiddlesticks.'

Van der Weijde restricted any further discussion to fashion, about which he knew very little, and life in Holland, which delighted the ladies and caused the Governor to sulk. Finally, the last rites of the evening were blessed with an exceedingly good port. The men tried to draw van der Weijde out on international affairs, but he diplomatically dodged the debate.

As the Governor walked van der Weijde to the door at the end of the evening he said, 'I've asked Christoffel Brand to arrange a meeting with you and young Chiron tomorrow. Come to the Castle at about 10 o'clock.'

Chapter 2
Abraham Chiron

'Abraham, did you hear Captain van der Weijde arrived on the *Paauw?*' asked Christoffel Brand before he got halfway into Abraham Chiron's office.

Abraham Chiron, a German, ran the trading operation that packaged and distributed produce brought in by farmers. Most was shipped to Holland, but enough was retained to supply the local market and passing ships.

'I know, I spoke to Captain Snyders,' replied Chiron. 'I know him well, he may even be joining the lodge and I have cargo for him. Who is van der Weijde anyway?'

'He calls himself Second Deputy Grand Master and Plenipotentiary and he has a commission from the Grand Master Baron van Boetzelaer to visit lodges abroad and receive communications and dues from them,' said Brand, taking a chair with one hand and sitting without being invited. 'The Governor has arranged a meeting with him for 10 o'clock this morning. You and I are to be there.'

'What does he want from us?'

'I don't know exactly, but he's convoked a meeting of Masons this coming Saturday at the Governor's house in the Castle. He seems a decent enough fellow. I told him you're our leader and he's anxious to meet you.'

'They've never bothered us before, but it's perhaps better late than never. I really think he wants to help, but he may not be pleased with what I've been doing here.'

'Look my friend, we're behind you. He only has power if we give it to him.'

'I suppose you're right. Let's get the blokes together and meet him. I'll try to see him on my own before Saturday in case there's trouble heading our way.'

The ten gathered at the Council Chamber attached to the Governor's residence in the Castle. It was quite relaxed as van der Weijde had taken the trouble of having a few words individually with each of them. He had arranged coffee and cakes and beckoned them around the big table, taking his own coffee with him.

'Brethren, I thank you for joining me here today. It's a delight to be back in Cape Town. I've had an opportunity to meet with Brother Abraham Chiron and we've agreed on how we should go forward from here.'

Chiron nodded in agreement.

'There've been big changes in Freemasonry in Holland and our Grand Master Baron Boetzelaer is keen to expand its influence throughout the Dutch world. As you may know, the Grand National Lodge of the United Netherlands has been in existence for years, but in many ways it was not much more than a province of the Grand Lodge of England. A little over a year ago the two grand lodges signed a convention whereby we'll remain good friends, but will now run our own affairs. I've been commissioned to visit brethren in far flung reaches who have connections with Dutch Freemasonry to place them on a firm footing and I've been empowered to help you sort out the necessary paperwork and issue provisional warrants.'

'As Brother Abraham has said, we've an opportunity to obtain a warrant from the Grand Lodge of the United Netherlands and I think we should welcome his offer and take it on in the bonds of friendship,' said Chiron. 'We've tried our best, but we've made some mistakes for which I apologise. Today we'll prepare a petition for such a warrant.'

'That's correct,' said van der Weijde.

'What will it cost?' asked O. G. de Wet.

'Seventy rixdollars should cover it,' said van der Weijde. 'I assure you if there's anything left over we'll deduct it from future dues.'

'Dues?' enquired de Wet.

'Ten rixdollars a member per year.'

'What do we get for that?'

'You'll be registered with the Grand Lodge, which will assist with administration and will look after your interests.'

They spent the rest of the morning filling in forms and at noon adjourned to a tavern at the harbour to celebrate and elect officers.

'I like the name Lodge de Goede Hoop,' piped Brand.

'Hear! Hear! Agreed,' the rest chirped in unison.

With a little wobble Brand rose to propose a toast, 'To our Master, Abraham Chiron, long may he live!'

'Hear! Hear!'

'I thank you for the toast,' said Chiron, rising. 'You all know that as the youngest amongst you I wanted someone with more authority to take on the mantle.'

'No! No! You're our man.'

'Before I sit I'd like to propose a toast to Brother Jacobus Alexander la Febre and Brother Pieter Soermans, my wardens. We now need to elect a secretary and treasurer.'

'I say Olaff; he's not here to object,' laughed Brand.

'I propose Jan Gie as secretary and Christoffel Brand as treasurer,' said Chiron, trying to maintain order.

A few days later, Chiron invited Christoffel Brand and his wife to join them for dinner with van der Weijde. Van der Weijde had gladly accepted as he liked Chiron, although he was some way above him on the social ladder. And his need to know more about him outweighed a venture across the social mores of Cape Town.

They set up the reception party on the stoep. Although they were on the street, the stoep was cool and they tried to catch as much of the breeze as they could while the setting sun kissed the top of the mountains. Marie Chiron was heavily pregnant and could not bear the kitchen, so Sissie Brand popped in and out to keep an eye on the *bredie* but Meitjie the slave girl seemed to have everything under control.

Van der Weijde was delighted to be welcomed to the Chiron's modest home. Always the gentleman, he lingered over the ladies' hands and breathed compliments which brought giggles from them. They sat in the corner of the stoep drinking the heavenly evening in, the ladies dominating Abraham for information about the latest fashions and gossip in Holland. When the women were finally summoned by Meitjie to the kitchen, the men grabbed their opportunity. The first discussion was, as always, about the unpleasantness of the voyage, with each trying to outdo the others with the uniqueness of their experiences.

Marie's call to dinner put an end to that discussion. She had gone to enormous trouble. Even though they were nudging the lower rungs of the social ladder she was going to show them, the Brands and the visitor, that they knew how to do things properly. The table was a silky yellowwood with homespun placemats and candles that twinkled off the glasses and silver. Blue-and-white Delft plates lay in little flat pyramids, the top one brimming with *boontjie sop* – bean soup with browned onions – that was served with chunky fresh bread and a jigger of brown sherry.

'Did you stay with the Nörthlings when you arrived?' enquired van der Weijde to make conversation and to find out as much as possible about the man he had entrusted with the new lodge.

'No, I stayed at the Castle barracks; it was awful,' laughed Chiron. 'But it got me off my backside to look for something better.'

'Is it difficult to make friends here in the Cape with its strict social laws?'

'Not really, being German and Lutheran I associated with that community. Further, Ryk Tulbach's refusal to accept our religion brought us closer together as we held house meetings to which the authorities turned a blind eye. It was at one of these that I met Martin Melck, who befriended me and invited me to his magnificent estate, Elsenburg. Perhaps he wanted to boast or had thoughts of marriage for his two daughters, who are homely. They became like the family I left behind in Europe to improve my position with the VOC. There's nothing like the experience you can get here with an enterprise that is also a government. Even though I've only been here a short while, I've been a trader, customs officer and been out on *burgherwacht*, a police force staffed by members of the Company and volunteers. Elizabeth Melck went out of her way to draw me into their circle and introduced me to many of her lady friends, which is where I was lucky enough to meet Marie Roger de Sedan.'

'My mother took an instant liking to him, but it took a while for my father to give his blessing,' said Marie. 'We married on 23 September 1770, almost a year to the day after his arrival.'

Sissie Brand came out of the kitchen carrying a steaming bowl, with Meitjie following with a dish of coarsely diced potatoes.

'*Waterblommetjie bredie*,' she announced.

The onions and lamb stew overlaid with *waterblommetjies* (water hyacinth flowers) that had slowly simmered all day with sorrel sent a heady aroma through the room. Marie laid a bed of diced potatoes on each plate and spooned over a generous helping of *bredie* with a crescent of peas from her own garden on the side all garnished with *blatjan* and freshly chopped onion. Van der Weijde tucked in with relish.

'Abraham, where did you become a Mason?' asked van der Weijde, wiping his mouth.

'In Frankfurt am Main. My Father insisted I join his lodge, Zur Einigkeit. I'm glad he did, so I was disappointed there was no Masonic lodge when I arrived in the Cape. At a Company function I met Christoffel Brand and while shaking hands I felt him seeking out my fingers. We declared our membership of the brotherhood and later he introduced me to Jan van Schoor, another company man, and Olaff de Wet, the Landdrost of Stellenbosch. The four of us started to initiate brethren.'

'We thought he was a bit of a dandy at first,' smiled Brand. 'He could easily have passed for a young Rembrandt, a wispy moustache over an ever-ready smile, a candid and direct gaze, a soft beret on his head, a fur collar to his cloak which covered all, leaving only enough of his rich silk shirt to impress. He bristled with energy, but had enough charm to dilute his latent arrogance.'

'I straightened him out,' laughed Marie. 'With a little help from Ryk Tulbach.'

'His enthusiasm compensated for his youth and inexperience,' continued Brand. 'It was difficult for this very young man to gather us older men around him, but we were happy to be led by him even though he was working a mishmash of mismatched degrees.'

'I was initiated in Germany and thought Freemasonry was the same everywhere,' explained Chiron. 'My colleagues here didn't know any better, so we worked the best ritual I could put together. But now that you're here you'll be able to give us direction.'

'Do you intend to stay long in Cape Town?' asked van der Weijde.

'We love it here; it's so different from Europe. I could never afford a home like this and a slave. I like to sit on the stoep where I have a glimpse of the sea, can smoke my pipe and greet the neighbours. Where can you do that in Frankfurt? And the food is very cheap.'

'But the lack of social life and the distance from head office, which makes promotion virtually impossible, must be frustrating.'

'For some it is. It leads to much drinking, which has become such a problem that van Plettenberg plans to further tax drink this year. This is why it is so important that Freemasonry takes hold here; it'll bring discipline and purpose to people.'

———•◆•———

There was no consecration or formal start to the lodge; they simply kicked off on 4 May 1772. They began by opening an Entered Apprentice Lodge, for which three candidates were proposed and balloted. That was closed soon afterwards and a Master Masons' Lodge was opened in which Brother Marthinus Adriaan Bergh, who was described as a 'Compagnon', was raised to the 'sublime degree of a Master Mason'. They then closed this and reopened the

Entered Apprentice Lodge and J. H. Stammer was initiated gratis and promptly employed for two rixdollars a month as the equivalent of our tyler, a watchman on the outer door.

Two of the new members, van Oudtshoorn and Captain Snyders, showed such promise that the lodge wrote off to the Grand Lodge to ask that their names be included in the final warrant. The lodge held eight meetings before July 1772, often two on one day, with as many as two or three workings at a meeting; then the minutes stopped for some unknown reason. Jan Gie did not become secretary, but rather the job was given to M. van Oorde, one of the new members. Shortly thereafter he resigned, but the lodge voted seven to four not to accept his resignation and appointed C. F. German as assistant secretary. From here little is known of the lodge as the next twenty pages of the minute book are blank, resuming only on 21 January 1774. It is clear that the lodge did not stop working during this period as new names were added to the roll and positions allocated.

⸻ • ⸻

'Abraham, did you hear that van der Weijde was killed?' yelled Christoffel Brand, trying to catch his breath as he burst into the Chiron's kitchen where the family were about to have breakfast.

'What happened?' asked Marie, shifting her baby son from one hip to the other.

'Nobody really knows. Van der Weijde was here on his way back to Holland from India and van Plettenberg invited him for dinner. I was also there, as was Philip Cassel, the captain of an English ship due to sail in two days. Everyone seemed to be enjoying themselves and the wine was flowing freely. At one point, though, the discussion became heated. I could not grasp what it was about as I was at the other end of the table. I think Cassel said we would be at war with the English soon or the French would be and we'd be involved, but I don't recall Abraham being in the discussion. Then it all cooled down and appeared to finish in peace and harmony. The two of them later walked home together up the Heerengracht where Hettie Hoenderdos heard a commotion. When she went out she found Abraham wounded on the ground and Cassel with sword in hand. She says the captain was in his cups. They took van der Weijde to the new hospital, but he died this morning. Cassel either can't remember or refuses to tell what happened.'

'That's terrible,' exclaimed Chiron. 'But as a senior servant of the Company I suppose they'll take care of arrangements.'

'But he was a Mason,' said Brand. 'It should be our responsibility.'

'I suppose so. As Master of the Lodge I'll have to arrange a Lodge of Sorrows,' frowned Chiron. 'I've never done one before. Do you know what to do?'

'A bit of an irony, isn't it?' observed Marie. 'He comes here to organise the lodge and nine months later he's the first one to be buried by it.'

——◆——

The most remarkable thing about the new lodge was the tremendous amount of work they got through, yet in numbers they remained quite small. We do not know exactly how many members there were, as the Secretary had a curious way of recording the minutes: 'All members present except...' Their lack of growth was a disappointment to Chiron and his brethren and more so to the Grand Lodge. A meeting in the *voorkamer* (lounge) of Chiron's house in Buitenkant Street was arranged.

'Brethren, Amsterdam has called for a report on the "disappointing progress" of our lodge,' opened Chiron quietly. 'I was hoping we could draft a reply. You know our records are in a mess so I asked Brother Christoffel to reconstruct them from his legendary memory, which he's done. To quote him, "They're in the main accurate but not without error."'

Brand was about to spread a sheet of paper on the coffee table when Marie brought in coffee.

Waving the paper in the air, Brand explained, 'Here is my list. I've put them in tables with dates and workings of who did what and so on. "Disappointing"? My eye! Do they know we've had nearly 130 workings in little over two years? I'll wager that no other lodge can claim that.'

'That's remarkable,' muttered the lawyer, Jan Gie, adjusting his monocle. 'I think they refer to our membership.'

'We have fifteen full members and two serving brethren,' read Brand from his paper.

'What's so bad about that?' asked Pieter Soermans. 'We started with seven.'

'Let's include those two facts,' suggested Chiron. 'We can also add that we've now got our own premises.'

'Do we need to tell them that we rent it from Lodewyk Pichtner for eighteen rixdollars a month?' added Gie.

'We've nothing to hide.'

'I'd like to point out the difficulties we have here at the bottom of Africa,' stated Chiron. 'Especially the warnings from the pulpit which have caused wives to persuade their husbands to hold aloof from Freemasonry. The clergy see us as a threat, not an asset.'

'Yes, we can include that, but I think any man who lets his wife stop him is no good to us anyway,' huffed Brand.

'I don't believe they understand our circumstances here,' said Olaf de Wet. 'Most of our initiates are just passing through – sailors, soldiers, Company people. We're putting through over fifty candidates a year, many of them noblemen, and battling to keep up with the other degrees. But then many of our achievements sail away.'

'Do you suggest we turn down transient men?' asked Chiron.

'Not at all. It's just that lodges elsewhere get the benefit of our good work. Some transient Freemasons have even progressed to the third degree here.'

'For me the biggest problem is that the Company here is not keen on us,' chipped in Soermans. 'Governor Ryk Tulbach's social laws are ludicrous and Grand Lodge should talk to him.'

'He'll die soon, he's very frail, which is why they appointed van Plettenberg as acting Governor. We can talk to him.'

'Good point,' nodded Chiron.

The last thing Chiron needed at this time was issues with the lodge. Trade was a worry, his division was doing moderately well, the world was crying out for what he had to offer, but shipping was a problem because of the English blockade of the Atlantic to protect their American interests. This had not affected him so far, but he could sense trouble on the horizon.

Local supplies were also becoming difficult; farmers did not grow much beyond Paarl and he had approached van Plettenberg – to no avail – to allow farming of the black ground that extended to Mossel Bay. But his old friend Olaf de Wet had been made his boss and he had received a promotion. De Wet agreed with his recommendation to distribute dried fruits and nuts and the strapping young second captain of the *Salomon*, François Duminy, had convinced him to think of honey, which never went off.

Although Duminy was French, Chiron had a lot in common with him. They were of the same age and Marie and Duminy's fiancée were friends. The next time he was in Cape Town Chiron had him initiated into Lodge de Goede Hoop.

Duminy was a foundling child left on convent steps and was christened François René after Good King René, the custodian of all orphans. But he did not know this until the day before he went to sea. The church had given little François to Antoine Lebre Duminy and his wife Anne. François knew his father had done many things, like growing wine and farming, but he only remembered him as Captain Duminy, commanding officer of the defences of Port Louis and Bayonne. He had a happy face even though his nose was red from the wine he so loved, but he could also be stern, particularly when he drilled his troops.

Duminy had always been fascinated by the sea and loved to sit on the Port Louis breakwater watching the waves roll in. It was a place of solace until the day before he left for sea, aged nine. After mass his adoptive parents revealed to him that they were not his real parents. His mother cried and twisted her handkerchief around her hand until the blood stopped.

'You are going to sea tomorrow and it is right that you know,' said his father bravely. 'When you were a baby the convent gave you to us and we have loved you like our own. You were baptised François René and we gave you our name. We would be proud if you would keep it. Tomorrow you will go to sea as a *volontaire* and you'll learn to be an officer. Uncle Pierre le Goff, your mother's brother, is the captain of a French East India Company ship. He owes me, so you'll be alright.'

Duminy and the other *volontaires* were schooled at sea as part of their apprenticeship. He excelled at navigational mathematics and loved the history and literature taught by the ship's surgeon. At the age of seventeen he was registered in the log book of the *Comte d'Argenson* as *pilot* (navigator). Two years later he transferred to the *Duc de Perthievre* also as *pilot*. In 1771 he was a second lieutenant on the French merchant vessel, *Cérès*, which docked in Cape Town. There he booked into Ben Nörthling's guesthouse and met the proprietor's very beautiful 14-year-old daughter, Johanna.

He loved to relate that he was not the only one attracted to her and that the French writer, Bernadin de Saint-Pierre, who also stayed with the Nörthlings, mentions her in his book. De Saint-Pierre wrote that they took a carriage from Newlands and describes the oak-lined roads and orchards heavily laden with fruit. The highlight of his trip was to climb Table Mountain to watch the sun rise.

He writes that on the top Johanna served them a refreshing drink of lemonade and Muscat wine and poured out her grief at the departure of her love. Duminy was sure she was referring to him.

Duminy returned to the Cape in 1773 and once again stayed with the Nörthlings. Johanna had blossomed into an even more beautiful young woman. He knew very little about women – especially refined, shy, cosseted young ladies – and he only spoke a little Dutch and she a little French. He tried to play his hand the best he knew and she promised to wait for him when again he set sail. In October 1776 he returned as second captain of the *Salomon*, where he met the famous explorer James Cook aboard the *Resolution*. They had much in common and Duminy was proud to tell him of their discovery of uncharted islands in the Maldives group, which they named the Salomon Islands after their ship. He liked Cook;

they were both interested in navigation, botany and zoology. No one could know that it was to be Cook's last voyage which ended in his death in Hawaii.

It was during Duminy's next visit, also in 1776, that Chiron again saw the giant Frenchman. He was down at the docks awaiting a shipment. By now he had received a further promotion and was in charge of all warehousing. When the *Bella Artur* docked from Madagascar he was surprised to see that it was captained by Duminy.

'*Mon ami!*' he boomed. '*Bon jour.*'

'*Allo* François.'

'I was delighted to see that I was carrying cargo for you, Abraham,' he roared. 'Bosun, unload Mynheer Chiron's cargo and be careful, his men are watching you. I'm going to take my friend for a brandy then we'll be back to inspect it. But be quick, I have my love waiting.'

'I must congratulate you on the captain's epaulettes,' said Chiron as they sat at a tavern.

'A fine little ship. I have Baron Benyowsky to thank for it. He sailed with me back to the Cape and I learnt so much from him.'

'I have heard of Benyowsky. Quite a character I understand. Does he own your boat?'

'No, he's a shareholder, but, as you say, a very complex character. You know he brought two slaves with him while being a champion of liberty? He's a friend of Benjamin Franklin's.'

'Franklin's a very senior Freemason. Is Benyowsky?'

'I don't know. He's never mentioned it.'

'I'm sure he is,' said Chiron. 'Why don't you come and eat with us tonight?'

'Abraham, I am a man in love. When I've finished this brandy I'm off to see her.'

'Bring her along.'

They arrived at about six with the sun still a fiery ball; a light breeze off the mountain cooled the air.

Chiron rose from his place on the stoep and put down his pipe, 'François, I can see why you're looking so marvellous.'

On his arm was Nörthling's daughter, and they did look good together, he in a new cloak, her eyes alive with mischief and secrets. Marie, hearing the greetings, came out with the children led by little Abraham and Pieter and carrying Ruth on her hip. Marie led Johanna and the children off while Chiron directed Duminy to a table of drinks. After pouring sherry they settled down with their pipes on the cushions laid out on the built-in bench, which was part of the party wall.

'We've got a nice little lodge here in Cape Town. You should think of joining.'

'I might at some time, but now I have a lot on my mind.'

As the lights went on over the town the men went inside to join the women, the roast lamb sending a warm fragrance through the house. Chiron was about to find out what it was on Duminy's mind.

'These two are to be married,' blurted Marie as they sat.

Duminy shrugged sheepishly, '22 February next year. You'll come of course.'

'I nearly turned him down when he told me he had to sail a week later,' said Johanna.

'I hate the idea, but now that I have a ship of my own I can't afford to lose it. It'll give me a chance to make enough money to buy us a home.'

Although Lodge de Goede Hoop was properly founded and was registered on the rolls of the Grand Lodge of the United Netherlands, it was still far from the homeland. Chiron was young, inexperienced and without high social standing. Nonetheless he ruled as Master with an intuitive wisdom, illustrated by a few extracts from the minutes

The lodge as always was very busy and many of the candidates were transient, so he introduced the practice of putting brethren through two degrees on the same evening. This often involved holding multiple meetings with different brethren. And he tried to introduce discipline by imposing fines for absenteeism and uncouth behaviour in the lodge. Where necessary he used his own judgement. In one instance a Captain de Veye confessed to performing a number of Masonic degrees 'on the desolate waves'. The lodge congratulated him for his diligence and promptly reworked them at a fee of 93 rixdollars each.

Chiron introduced a new class of membership – a serving brother. Being initiated in the lodge did not mean automatic membership and a brother had first to prove himself. The period of serving brotherhood was a probationary period in which the initiate had to look after the buildings as well as see to catering. The first two serving brothers, Hellberg and Deeg, were very busy men and so the lodge proposed to buy its first slave as part of its fixed property. The motion was apparently not passed, as a fortnight later it was agreed to hire a young slave for three rixdollars a month to help the serving brethren.

A curious thing from the early minutes of Lodge de Goede Hoop was the issue of slaves. In November 1775, we read, 'It was decided to sell the lodge's slave for not less than 160 rixdollars – and buy another.' And so Slammet was sold for 170 rixdollars.

At the next meeting a new slave from Ceylon was offered to the lodge and they took him on approbation for a month, then bought him for 155 rixdollars. In May 1776 he was sold to the serving brethren and two more were bought. The two serving brethren at the time, Brother Hellberg and Brother Deeg, argued about their rights to these two slaves. Tired of the bickering, the lodge sold each of them one of its slaves and ended the lodge's ownership of slaves for a number of years.

Considering the ethos of Freemasonry it is astounding to learn the lodge bought, kept and sold slaves. And it is a heavy indictment that only one slave is actually recorded by name. But this is nothing in comparison to the actions of François Duminy who supplemented his income by trading in slaves. A captain in the merchant navy was not well paid, but was permitted to trade on his own behalf. Soon after meeting Chiron in 1776 he was given command of the much larger *Deodat*, which he used to trade in coffee, spices and slaves with money lent to him by French merchant J. B. Monnier. From the proceeds he was able to buy a house on Kerkplein for his new wife and a nearby plot between Long, Hout and Castle streets.

Chiron was again promoted by the VOC and given more responsibility. After five years as Master he felt he needed to hand over the reins and in June 1777 the senior warden, Brother Jan Coenraad Gie was elected to the position. The lodge did not bother with any formal installation: 'The Worshipful Retiring Master rose from his eminent chair and welcomed his successor in his place, wishing him strength, happiness, enlightenment out of the East, and that he might above all increase in the royal art of Masonry'... The brethren decided to celebrate the day by themselves with a supper and 'without a ball'.

Gie continued where Chiron left off and at the March meeting the following year Captain François Renier Duminy, 'The French Candidate', was initiated. In the same month they had five meetings, eight initiations, eight passings and five raisings. Any lodge today would be happy to have that amount of work over four or five years, yet only Burgers and Duminy became full members. Daniel Brand followed Gie as Master and got off to a flying start, to be crowned by an amazing December with five meetings, sixteen degrees and sumptuous dinners as well as table lodges. Yet there was something seriously wrong at the lodge. At the January 1779 meeting 'the Master complained bitterly of the lamentable state of the lodge.' They limped along, churning out candidates, but membership dwindled to ten.

Chiron rounded up the members to discuss the problems, but they could not put their finger on the malaise. Christoffel Brand reported that 'in the eight years they had been going they had had 240 candidates and were reduced to ten full members. Where were they? In England, in the East, France, Germany, dead, anywhere but in Cape Town.' One of the most serious issues concerned social strains. At the January 1779 meeting, the Master 'exhorted the Past Masters and wardens to put an end to all disputes over rank, and to discountenance ambition, self seeking, and ill-feeling towards others.' This arose out of a curious social revolution taking place in Cape Town at the time. Everyone either worked for the Company or were free burghers. Employees were arranged in a strict grading system on strict pay scales, which encouraged social competition that filtered into the burgher community; everyone in the colony was extremely conscious of their rank and importance. Rules of social conduct were carefully documented and promulgated by Tulbach, not unlike the rules of etiquette developed by Beau Nash in Bath earlier in the same century. These rules attempted to regulate the conduct of every level of society: who could wear what, who could own different carriages, who could live where. Time and again the Governor was called in to settle disputes over who took precedence in church or whose chairs were to be placed nearest to the pulpit. While Freemasonry promoted equality, lodges were full of ranks and precedence and many joined for that reason, only to find it held no real social advantage and left soon after. This was having a serious effect on the lodge: of the 188 names listed by Brand, only forty-one became members and six became serving brothers.

Some believed the lodge was doing nothing wrong, others were not convinced, but they all agreed that their fortunes were being affected by the situation in the Atlantic, which was becoming tenser. England, trying to protect their American interests, declared their sovereignty over the Atlantic, which upset the French who ended up playing tag with the English Navy all over the Atlantic; the English responded by unleashing privateers on French vessels.

Holland was allied with England, but after being subjugated by the French, they became enemies. A British brig in Table Bay in March 1781 was seized by van Plettenberg and renamed the *Postillion* (the postman). Duminy, the most experienced captain in Cape Town, was offered its command as well as responsibility for the harbours at Table Bay and False Bay. He was tired of being away from his growing family, of being at sea for months at a time, and looked forward to short costal trips and more time at home. He jumped at the offer of a five year contract with the VOC at sixty guilders a month.

After the outbreak of the American War of Independence in 1778, in which France sided with the colonists, the French and the English realised the strategic value of the Cape. They set off in a race to occupy it. The British fleet, under Admiral Johnstone, was surprised by his French counterpart, Admiral de Suffren, at the Cape Verde islands and was defeated. The French then made a dash for the Cape and landed 3 000 troops 'to assist the Governor' in 1781. This left van Plettenberg and his advisers in a quandary as the commander of his own forces, Colonel Robert Gordon, was muscled aside and lines of command were confused.

The 'French-help' turned into a virtual coup-d'état. Van Plettenberg did not trust the French and decided to salvage what he could and loaded five ships with the most valuable goods to send back to Holland. The first part of his plan went off without a hitch, and they slipped quietly out of Cape Town under French noses. However, he had not taken the English into account. After their bruising at Cape Verde they came bustling down the coast spoiling for a fight and found the Dutch ships, capturing four and sinking one. This had a disastrous effect on the fortunes of the VOC and began their slide towards bankruptcy.

Duminy might have been looking for a quiet life, but van Plettenberg had other ideas; he felt it was vital to inform the Company's trading partners and representatives in the East and dispatched Duminy to Cochin, Malabar and Colombo, giving him no more than a week to prepare the ship. His budget was 3 000 rix-dollars for provisions and he had no time to turn it into a trading voyage. Except for being fired upon as they approached Colombo, mistaken for freebooters, the trip went off fairly well. Arriving back in Cape Town he found the place in an uncomfortable confusion and the lodge in serious decline.

Chiron was beginning to hate his job. He and Marie loved the Cape, but he had a new boss appointed by the French who placed intolerable pressure to direct every transaction in their favour. Then, for no apparent reason, the French pulled out. At about this time a fleet of ten Dutch ships arrived in Cape Town in the most terrible circumstances with over a thousand of its compliment dead. Van Plettenberg decided to send Duminy and the *Postillon* to Holland to update the VOC on the situation. The Governor must have agonised over the decision to send a French captain on a Dutch ship which he had stolen from the English through the English blockade of the Atlantic. They dreamed up a consignment of goods for Simpson and Company in London so that he could pretend he was working for them. He sailed on 28 December 1783, which was the last time Duminy would see Chiron and Marie.

We cannot be sure if there were any more meetings of the lodge. The main membership dwindled and Chiron had grown disillusioned with the lodge and his job. In addition, his father had grown weak and wanted him to come home to run the family business. He left the Cape with his family and took the lodge's warrant with him back to Holland in 1784 and it was struck off the roll of the Grand Lodge of the United Netherlands on 16 October of that year.

Chapter 3
François Renier Duminy

Johanna was at the dock holding a new bundle they had christened Margretha Arnoldina Victoire. François Antoine Benjamin was trying to escape from Thibault, and the slave Platfoet, was running after Jeanne, who was now five years old. Where were Abraham and Marie? The mighty *De Meermin*, with her beautiful mermaid figurehead and twenty-two guns bristling on her sides, effortlessly slid into her berth. Her captain, François Duminy, waved his hat festooned with three-foot ostrich feathers. He did not bother with the gang plank and swung to the dock, hugging and kissing Johanna and the brood. It seemed as if everyone in Cape Town had turned out on 6 April 1784 to see the Company's new ship.

When they got home, Johanna fussed as she settled Duminy into his favourite chair with his pipe and cool lager. She lifted his feet onto a pouffe, wanting him to herself, but there was no way of keeping her parents and the children away.

'We were so worried about you, tell us what happened,' said Oupa Nörthling.

'Perhaps some other time,' suggested Johanna.

'It's a long story,' smiled Duminy, exhaustion etched on his face but itching to recount his adventures.

Van Plettenberg sent Duminy on the *Postillon* to Holland to bring head office up to date with the situation of their fleet in the Cape and in the East. The plan was to dock at l'Orient in France, avoid the English Channel, and make his way across land to Amsterdam. He set sail on 17 December 1782 and was blessed with good weather, which was perfect for anticipating Admiral Johnston and the British fleet. He managed to dodge them until just before he reached his destination where he ran into them on 17 February 1783. He threw his dispatches overboard and surrendered, thankful that no one recognised the *Postillon* as their own *Betsy*.

'I was captured and taken a prisoner of war to Saint Lucia in the West Indies,' recounted Duminy. 'I explained to Johnston that whereas I was born in France I had been living in the Cape and was an agent for John Simpson in London. My cargo was his and they had no right to seize it. Well, they held me for a while as they didn't know what to do with a Frenchman with goods for an Englishman and I eventually persuaded them to take me to London where I could be of some use to them.'

Duminy and what remained of his cargo, which included two slaves, was taken to Britain on the *Sandwich*. By the time he delivered the goods to Simpson he was short 2 299 guilders, which he could not pay. This did not please Simpson, but the rest of London took a liking to him. He gave an interview to the *London Daily Advertiser* about the wreck of the Grosvenor and filled in details of the Battle of Cape Verde. He created such a good impression they let him go to Holland, where he expected trouble. On the contrary, the Hollanders welcomed him with open arms. The French were equally happy to see him and even awarded him the Chevalier Grand Cross of the Order of St Philippe.

'But you've never been interested in rank,' stated Duminy's

mother-in-law.

'Yes and no,' replied Duminy. 'I was concerned at my vulnerable position, being French employed by the Dutch, so I took the award to enhance my prestige.'

The VOC ordered a new 500-ton, 115-foot ship, *De Meermin*, fitted with twenty-two guns. Duminy was given command, which meant he had to stay longer in Europe than he would have wished as he had to oversee construction. It also provided him with the opportunity to visit his ageing step-parents in Port Louis and advance his Masonic position. He took the degrees of *Chevalier of the Religious Order of St John of Jerusalem Palestine Rhodes* and *Rose Croix*, which meant he could call himself Sovereign Prince Rose Croix. And he persuaded the High Chapter of the Netherlands to appoint him Inspector General, which automatically made him head of the Masonic Order in the Cape. The ship took five months to build and was launched from the Texel Shipyards, from where it escorted six of the Company's ships to the Cape. On board was a detachment of de Meuron's Swiss mercenaries.

Johanna called the party to dinner. The candles were ablaze in their new home, which was a source of great pride to Johanna. They had bought it before François left, but she had added its life – yellow and stinkwood furniture, Cape silver and Delft china. Meisie the slave maid had made brown soup, crayfish dripped with lemon butter and grilled on the coals, and a fig pudding. Served with claret, it was everything that François loved and had missed on his adventure.

'Tell me about Abraham and Marie,' said Duminy.

'After you left for France, Chiron became more and more depressed,' responded Johanna. 'I think he began to hate the Company and its "nonsense", as he called it. The lodge was failing, and he felt responsible. One day they came to tell me they were going home to Germany. When they left, the lodge was not working, so he took the warrant with him.'

'I'll have to get it back again.'

De Meermin

Duminy had been appointed Inspector General of Freemasonry by the Grand Lodge of the United Netherlands to keep a supervisory eye out over Masonry in the Cape, but there was no Masonry to supervise. Lodge de Goede Hoop had faltered and it was his duty to get it going again. But there were other forces which took control of his life before he could do so.

Governor van Plettenberg was under pressure and the VOC had decided to replace him. Duminy had scarcely been home for a few days when van Plettenberg, in a last gasp attempt to sweeten his own position, ordered Duminy to ready *De Meermin* to sail for Madagascar to collect a shipment of rice and between 250 and 300 slaves. Johanna was furious.

'So much for the Dutch prohibition of the sale of slaves,' she snapped. 'It's so unfair. You've just come back after nearly two years.'

But Duminy was also in a difficult position; his superiors still had some doubts about his last trip and there had been some not-so-veiled threats that he might lose command of his new ship. And the tides and winds were favourable. So he agreed and took with him a bright young Swedish clerk, Anders Stockenström, who would go on to become Governor of the Cape. They arrived in Madagascar on 9 August to find no slaves available.

They headed for Mozambique where he managed to buy 316 slaves, mostly young men with some women and children. By the time he returned to Cape Town on 12 January 1785, 105 of these had died. This was considered good as a 50% survival rate was factored into the trade and Duminy was rewarded with a bonus which was partly paid in slaves.

To make the most of his new ship and its captain, van Plettenberg appointed Duminy as harbourmaster of both Table Bay and Simon's Bay with the additional responsibility of charting the waters around the Cape and further afield as well as undertaking the occasional patrol. Duminy was delighted at the prospect of settling down to a more stable life and jumped at the opportunity. Five months later his ship and *De Meeuwtje* were sent to find two other VOC ships. In this they failed, but they did buy 345 slaves and only lost 50. This was the last of his slave-trading voyages.

The following year he was asked to prepare a report, 'The Slave Trade in the Indian Ocean'. He was specifically asked to address the mortality rate on board. He reported that most of the deaths were from dysentery as a result of the appalling way they were kept by Arab dealers, and that many were already infected when they came on board. His solution was to keep the ship scrupulously clean by washing it down with vinegar every day because once the disease took hold one could lose the entire compliment. On many ships smallpox was an issue, though he never came across it. The next biggest killer was depression and he advocated sympathy and care by moving batches of slaves around in open air.

———•———

After the French forces evacuated the Cape, the VOC decided to shore up the defences of their possession and replaced van Plettenberg with Lieutenant-Colonel Cornelis Jacob van der Graaff, a military strategist and expert on military fortifications. Duminy's advice was to become invaluable on Cape sea routes as he knew the coast better than anyone else and he was appointed Equipage Master, one of the highest ranks in the Cape administration, with responsibility for the whole coastline, imports and exports, and harbours. Van der Graaff also asked him to develop the timber industry in Plettenberg Bay, facilitate grain production in Swellendam and Mossel Bay, establish trade with Walvis Bay and oversee expeditions of explorers to evaluate the hinterland.

Duminy took to his new job with vigour. He negotiated deals with woodcutters in Plettenberg Bay, built the woodsheds that are there to this day, set in place controls against unplanned and over-cutting of trees, and took out the first load of timber in August 1788. He set up grain sheds in Mossel Bay and continued charting the coast. François le Valliant, the young French explorer who met him at this time, described him as tall and elegant with his Chevalier Star on his breast and harbourmaster's epaulets on his shoulders. His purple silk cloak, now in the South African Cultural Museum, shows him to be over 6' 3".

But not everyone was impressed. Local detractors accused Duminy of paying van der Graaff 50 000 guilders for the job, which was impossible on his salary and circumstances. They claimed that there were equally qualified Dutchmen and regular churchgoers who could do the job. Moreover, he was a Catholic and a Freemason. These criticisms were hollow: he was married in the Dutch Reformed Church and never made an overt display of his Catholicism and the lodge at this time was not even functioning. Jealousy and growing resentment of the French was the probable cause of this backlash. Van de Graaff was even blamed for the minor revolution in Graaff-Reinet.

A delegation was sent to Holland about Duminy's appointment and to his great disappointment the Heeren XVII refused to ratify it. Nonetheless, van der Graaff did manage to keep him as master of False Bay harbour and captain of *De Duifie*. Notwithstanding, this was a prosperous time for Duminy and he used the proceeds from his trading operations to buy a two-morgen stand above the

Company Gardens and engage his friend Louis Michel Thibault to design a house on it, *le Jardin*, of which there are two drawings in Museum Afrika. He also bought the farm *Compagniesdam* and later two more, *Bokkerivier* and *Kykoedie*. In addition, being relieved of his duties as Equipage Master gave him the time to attend to his Masonic responsibilities.

━━◆━━

'*Allo! Allo!*' greeted Thibault, stepping onto the stoep with Evert van Schoor, one of the founders of the Lodge de Goede Hoop and father of a daughter Thibault was dating. Thibault had joined the lodge just before it had closed.

'Come sit in the courtyard, it's cooler there,' said Duminy, leading them through the house. 'The others will be along shortly.'

The courtyard was paved with a small fish pond in the corner and enclosed with a grapevine. Johanna appeared soon, bearing a tea tray.

'Did you know Louis and Elizabeth are to be married?' she blurted.

'What? How wonderful,' enthused Duminy as others began to arrive. Wanting to get on with business, he turned to van Schoor. 'Evert, I'm sorry the lodge closed down. What happened?'

'I agreed with Abraham Chiron. There were so few of us who came. There were lots of visitors and we conferred many degrees, but the response from residents was poor. Most of the problem was because of the rigid social structure here and religious attitudes. Because of equality in the lodge this was anathema to many officials. But there was also the problem with the French occupation, of which the only positive was that Louis joined.'

'I arrived after the French occupation,' objected Thibault.

By now most of the brethren had arrived and found seats in the courtyard where Johanna gave them refreshments and koeksusters.

'Look, brethren, it's time we started the lodge again,' said Duminy, opening the meeting.

'A few years ago Louis and Jan van Schoor spoke about starting it again, but somehow we never did,' added Christoffel Brand. 'You and the rest of us have lived through troubled times.'

'Yes, we got rid of the French then they changed governors,' said Duminy. 'De Graaff made me Equipage Master and I was running round the country doing all sorts of things.'

'Good things,' chipped in de Wet. 'You sorted out the timber industry and the wheat growers.'

'Then I got fired,' snorted Duminy.

'Bloody shame,' exclaimed Brand.

'You did well,' confirmed Burgers.

'We must avoid the problems that haunted us before the break-up,' said Duminy. 'I think we must make the lodge more attractive.'

'How?' asked de Smidt.

'We need a place where brethren can go for a drink, meet friends, perhaps play skittles or billiards. I think we need more social days with fine dinners and music.'

'Will we make it easier to become a member?' asked Brand

'No, I don't think so. We must keep up standards, but make it more desirable.'

'It'll cost a rich rixdollar,' said van Schoor.

'I guess it will,' concurred Duminy. 'I think we should each lend the lodge fifty rixdollars to get it started.'

'When will we get it back?' asked Brand.

'I don't know, but I'm prepared to advance an extra 100 rix-dollars for a billiard table,' offered Duminy.

'Do we need to get our warrant back?' asked Thibault.

'I don't think so. We should carry on as before and change later if needs be.'

Duminy was elected Master and so Lodge de Goede Hoop started again in 1794, albeit in an irregular way. One of its first candidates was the young assistant fiscal (public prosecutor) John Andries Truter.

⎯⎯•⎯⎯

The lodge started to function again in the only way it knew how: with many candidates, but few of them taking an active part. Their newest member, J. A. Truter, was an exception and he became deeply committed to Freemasonry. With his intellect and enthusiasm mixed with wisdom and charm he soon started to infuse a new spirit. It was exactly what was needed in the politically confused Cape. Britain was at war with France. France had overrun Holland and formed the Batavian Republic, which was forced to be pro-French and therefore at odds with the English. While the French had left, the Cape was now under the Batavians who had been nurtured by the French Revolution. The Dutch Royal House of Orange were in exile in England and were encouraging the British to take over the Cape before this strategic station again fell into the hands of the French.

Admiral Elphinstone was sent to take the Cape; this time he had no trouble from the French navy and he anchored in False Bay in 1795. He first tried negotiating a peaceful settlement, which was not to be, so he finally attacked and quickly overcame the token resistance. W. C. M. de Lille, in charge of defences and the warden of the lodge, was vilified for his early retreat and even charged with treason, but the charge was dismissed. Nevertheless, he resigned from the lodge and later committed suicide.

Major General Craig was made acting Governor until Lord Macartney took over. The new administration was more than happy to leave most of the VOC officers in place, but there were loyalty issues, especially with French officers. Thibault was very vocal about selling out to the enemy and would have nothing to do with them; Duminy was in too sensitive a position and was dismissed. Suddenly he had no source of income, his farms were hardly producing and he was forced to mortgage his homes and farms to keep up his lifestyle. Yet he showed no resentment toward the occupying power for his lack of employment and the setback to his fortunes.

As Master of the lodge, Duminy invited Elphinstone and Craig to attend meetings and offered them his gavel, a high Masonic courtesy to a senior Mason, and both became honorary members. Duminy made every effort to make English Masons welcome; this went a long way to help ease relationships in the Cape. In these un-settled times the lodge was doing well. The sculptor Anton Anrieth was proposed by Thibault and initiated in 1798. He would go on to play a huge part in the culture of the Cape.

Duminy, however, was feeling his age and in 1798 withdrew his candidacy for Master on health grounds. The following year he resigned as a member, spending more and more time taking mineral baths. While he suffered physically and financially, the same did not apply to the lodge which was in rude health from the patronage brought by military occupation. Truter was elected the new Master and he had very high aims for Freemasonry.

The Treaty of Amiens of March 1802 involved the handing back of the Cape to the Batavian Republic. They sent out Abraham de Mist, Baron of Uitenhage, as Commissioner-General together with J. W. Janssens to reform it. Not only was de Mist a Mason, but a very senior one with the title Deputy Grand Master National and he did a lot for Masonry in the short time he was at the Cape. He brought it back in line with mainstream Masonry and appointed Truter as the Deputy Grand Master National in his place when he left. This must have been a bitter blow to Duminy who felt he was owed the position. De Mist's reason was that Duminy's age and failing health would prevent him from continuing in office.'

In a civil capacity de Mist reinstated Duminy in his old job as harbourmaster of False Bay, a position which carried with it a house and helped Duminy get back on his feet. But gout, high blood pressure and arteriosclerosis continued to take their toll and he increasingly sought solace in laudanum and mineral baths. In 1806 the British fleet landed in Table Bay near Duminy's farm and retook the Cape. They were particular about keeping most of the former administration staff, but dismissed Duminy. This time he did resent their invasion, and it led to more financial woes. His beloved Joanna died in 1807 and he followed her in 1811.

Part 2

Lodge de Goede Hoop

Chapter 4
Sir John Andries Truter

'Brethren, I thank you for the confidence you have placed in me,' said John Andries Truter after the Director of Ceremonies announced he had been elected the Master of Lodge de Goede Hoop in 1798. 'I am conscious that I am a young Mason, but I'm ready to work for you, and I'll need your help and faith in me. I would be grateful if the senior brethren would meet with me to discuss our way forward straight after this meeting.'

To them he said, 'I thank you for joining me after one of the most important evenings of my life. Together we'll take this lodge to heights no other lodge in the world has ever reached. For this I think there are things we should take into account, movements we should control and a dream we should achieve together. We must raise our standards to achieve higher goals for Freemasonry; we must get our paperwork in order and our Warrant restored to us. I look to my dear friend and Brother, François Duminy, the Inspector General, to help us. Brother Thibault, I want you to help him and mentor the process.

'The irregular lodges which we've allowed to be formed, such as Lodge de Goede Trouw, must be regularised. We gave them a warrant without having a regular one ourselves, but we must support them without letting them forget which is the senior lodge in this part of the world. We must also be ever ready to welcome English brethren with open arms, although language is a difficulty. Having said that, we have granted them a dispensation to form a lodge they propose to call Africa No. 1, provided it obtains the consent of the Illustrious Protector. This it has done and was formed as No. 1 at the Cape of Good Hope.'

A few evenings later Truter invited Duminy, Cristoffel Brand and their wives to dinner. The dining room was decorated with yellowwood furniture, brass ornaments and candles that lit the dark pictures on the walls. The legendary cook, Meitjie, had prepared mushroom, leek and barley broth, venison stew with prunes, and brandied peaches, all served with Hendrik Cloete's wines.

'Oom François, we know you've resigned from the lodge, but we don't want to lose you,' said Truter.

'I'm an old man and it's time.'

'Nonsense, François, you're younger than me,' interjected Brand.

'You know he loves you, John, but the pain talks to him in the morning,' replied Johanna.

'It was because of you, Oom François, that I joined,' pleaded Truter. 'I know your fortunes have not been as fair as you'd have liked under the British, but we don't want to lose you for a few rixdollars. We'll rally behind you.'

Truter, who was born in 1763, had fond memories of this dining room. It was here that his uncle, O. G., president of the Council of Justice, announced during a meal of lambout followed by bread–and-butter pudding, that he had raised a subscription for him to study law at the University of Leyden.

The university, established by William of Orange, was larger than the whole of Cape Town and his head must have swirled as he walked in the footsteps of Rembrandt along streets lined with elegant buildings three to four stories high. He registered there in 1783 and four years later received a doctorate for his thesis *De Regula Civilus Juris Heredetarii: a semetipso non legator*. Though he could have remained in Europe, he chose to return because his future wife, Sophia de Wet, was waiting for him. They were married on 22 November 1789 in the Hoog Kerk. When he got back, he joined the VOC as an assistant in the fiscal's office and in 1793 was promoted to secretary of the Council of Justice with the rank of Deputy Merchant. His growing family first rented a house in Long Street while building their home, but later moved back to the family home when his parents decided to go wine farming in Stellenbosch.

Shortly after his appointment, Truter was sent with a commission as acting landdrost (magistrate) to investigate the disturbances in Graaff-Reinet. It appeared an innocuous enough brief, but this was a real baptism of fire, akin to sending in the greenhorn to clean up Dodge City. The Boers had been edging away from the Cape in a gradual but determined way, driven by fiercely independent ideals and disenchantment with the VOC. They did not accept the grudging way the Company allocated land that was not theirs to apportion and the lack of protection from Cape Town although they were expected to pay taxes. They could look after themselves and wanted their own republic.

Into this cauldron came Truter. He held meetings in the school hall and explained how they should work together. But the fractious burghers, bristling with arms, were only interested in discussing taxes and loaded him onto his horse and chased him back to the city. Leyden had not prepared him for this lesson. The following year things began to look up when he received a letter:

> John Andries Truter   2 June 1794
> You are invited to meet the Brethren of Lodge de Goede
> Hoop at the home of Chevalier François René Duminy,
> Inspector General of the Grand Lodge of the United
> Netherlands,
> le Jardin
> On Friday inst at four thirty.

'What do you make of it?' asked Sophia.

'I don't know. There was a lodge here ten years ago by that name, but it closed down about the same time as the French occupation. I'll go and find out.'

Truter paced himself to arrive at exactly four thirty, knowing exactly where Duminy's house was above the Company Gardens. Thibault had done a wonderful job of the home with the saddle of mountain as a backdrop. *Le Jardin* had simple lines with a serried row of arches shading the lower floor and providing a terrace for the upper level. There were several carriages in the circular outer court when he arrived and rapped the brass knocker. The door was opened by Johanna.

'Ah, Mynheer Truter, the captain is expecting you,' she greeted, indicating a door off the entrance hall to the library.

The giant Frenchman was behind his writing table with six other men in the room, most of them familiar to him. There was Christoffel Brand, Olaf de Wet, Zorn from the accounting office, de Lille who was head of defences, and Thibault sitting next to his father-in-law, Evert van Schoor.

'We've been meeting over the past few weeks with a view to starting Lodge de Goede Hoop again,' opened Duminy, after Truter had taken a seat. We have set the date for this – 24 June – and your uncle-in-law, Olaf, has suggested you may wish to join us.'

'You will be our first candidate,' nodded de Wet.

'It sounds interesting and I subscribe to your ethos, but I must inform you that I'll be away for a good part of the year and I don't want to let you down.'

'Olaf has explained that to us.'

Lodge de Goede Hoop

At the age of 31 Truter was initiated into Lodge de Goede Hoop, loving the measured way their ancient rituals unfolded to reveal lessons in being a better person. Scarcely had he joined than the Cape was again in turmoil when the British occupied it in 1795. This brought Lord Macartney as Governor, of whom Lady Anne Barnard writes, 'No public servant ever left office with purer hands.' She explains that when he took over the administration he 'trod very carefully and retained the Dutch Officials in their posts.' He dismantled the VOC monopolies on wheat, wine and livestock, leading to increases in production and prices. He retained Roman Dutch Law and Truter in his position.

Lady Ann Barnard's letters give a taste of the time. She was the oldest daughter of James Lindsay, the fifth Earl of Balcarres. Once wealthy and powerful, the family had lost nearly everything when the fourth Earl supported the Jacobite revolt of 1715. A great beauty, Lady Anne joined her sister in London while still in her twenties. 'There the two sisters lived together for many years,' writes WH Wilkens in the memoir included in a book of Lady Anne's letters.

> The beauty of Lady Margaret, and the charm and lively conversation of Lady Anne, 'one of the most fascinating women of her time,' as a contemporary describes her, made them very popular, and their house became a social centre , and a favourite resort of some of the most famous literary and political men of the day. Pitt, Burke, Sheridan, Windham, and Dundas are a few of those who were wont to avail themselves of the sisters' simple yet charming hospitality; the Prince of Wales was also one of their frequent guests, and his friendship with Lady Anne lasted all his life.
>
> With such opportunities Lady Anne, it may readily be believed, had many offers, some of them exceptionally good, but she refused them all. The reason that she remained unwed all these years is ascribed by her nephew, Colonel Lindsay, to indecision and a reluctance

to leave her sister... Then in 1793 she astonished her friends by marrying Andrew Barnard, son of the Bishop of Limerick. The marriage, from a worldly point of view, could hardly be considered other than imprudent. Lady Anne was forty-three years of age, her husband fifteen years her junior; he had been in the army; he was good looking, well mannered, of moderate ability and amiable disposition. It is only fair to say that, despite the disparity of age, he made Lady Anne a very good husband, and she grew to be much attached to him. The problem of ways and means early presented itself. Barnard had a small patrimony and many debts; Lady Anne had little or nothing.

Lady Anne solved this problem by getting her closest friend, Henry Dundas, the secretary for war and the colonies in Pitt's cabinet, to secure Andrew a position in Government. This led to Andrew landing the job of secretary of the colony during the first British occupation of the Cape. While this on the surface appeared below his station, there was an incentive. The wife of the Governor, Lord Macartney, had decided to stay in England and Lady Anne was designated First Lady. The couple arrived on 4 May 1797, and as Macartney chose not to live in the Castle, the Barnards were allocated the largest house in the complex. She immediately set about stamping her style on the place.

From the Castle of Good Hope, situated within the garrison, over which towers the Table Mountain at a considerable real distance (the close apparent vicinity being from the effect of its height), and from the window of my bed-chamber, which overlooks a colonnade built around a spacious pond of water supplied from the head and tail of a spouting dolphin, I begin this letter to my dearest Friend, firmly assured that he will be as much interested in its contents from private affection to the writer, as from curiosity to know every point, however minute, which regards a public concern,' she wrote to Dundas. 'Our house is a palace, containing such a suite of apartments as makes me fancy myself a princess when in it. I have had it fitted all up in the style of a comfortable, plain, English house. Scotch carpets, English linen, and rush-bottom chairs, with plenty of lolling sofas, which I have had made by regimental carpenters and stuffed by regimental tailors. In a week or two I shall invite all who wish to be merry without cards or dice, but who can talk, or hop to half a dozen black fiddlers, to come and see me on my public day, which shall be once a fortnight, when the Dutch ladies (all of whom love dancing, and flirting still more) shall be kindly welcomed, and the poor ensigns and cornets shall have an opportunity of stretching their legs as well as the generals. I shall not be stinted for room, as I have a hall of sixty feet, a drawing-room of forty, a dining-room of twenty, a tea-room of thirty, and three supper-rooms – in one of which only I shall have supper, and that cold and desultory, with sideboards and no chairs, as I wish to make my guests happy without being ruined by their drinking half a hogshead of claret every party. Ducks and chickens, etc, they shall have, but as turkeys are one pound apiece, I shall not fly at any of their excellencies.

Macartney resolved the problems of governance while Lady Anne was let loose on the elite. As she put it:

> The balls and parties were left for me to settle as I thought best. Mr Barnard wished me to consult the Fiscal to the proper mode of inviting the Dutch ladies. When I went down the list he threw in so many objections to persons whom he called 'disaffected' that I feared none would be left and said so. 'But remember,' I said, 'we are come not to call the righteous but to sinners to repentance.' 'Well,' he said, 'if you are determined to bring the sheep and the goats into one fold you must take the chance of your party becoming a bear-garden.' 'But I am going to give a ball,' I said. '*Mon ami*, music hath charms to soothe the savage beast.' He laughed and gave way and so I had things the way I wished.

In the same letter she says that many of the Dutch men were sulking, but the ladies enjoyed themselves: 'to plough with Heifers has always been reckoned a good means to improve reluctant soil' is how she put it.

The Barnards' tenancy ended rather bitterly when Sir George Yonge replaced Macartney as Governor. But there was still time for a few parties before they moved from the Castle to the cottage, *Paradise*, in Newlands. 'After we had waited, as one is duty bound, till General Fraser, our [acting] Commander-in-Chief, had given the first dinner to the Governor, we invited him here,' she wrote to Dundas.

Being desirous to influence the future invitations of Sir George by showing him a company composed of many of those who are attached to government, I wrote notes to many of the most democratic of my Beauties and their families, saying that, as the new Governor and his family were to be with us in the evening, I wished to present my old friends to the new. The effect was all I could desire – everyone came, and I had a splendid assembly. Sir George fell directly in love with the daughter of one of the greatest Jacobins in the place, as it was once supposed, though it was otherwise proved, and flirted as if he had been twenty-five. On the other hand, having observed, as I told you before, that there was a strong tendency amongst the higher military powers to exclude the subordinate officers from all share in pleasant dances or parties, I hinted to the colonels to bring all their ensigns and lieutenants, that they might appear in one civil house by way of a precedent, if that was anything. They thanked me and came. Of course, there was a handsome company, and as many supped as could find chairs. I presented my Dutch ladies to the Governor, and to his niece, Mrs Blake. They were surprised at their number and smart appearance.

The Thursday after, Mr Barnard invited fifty-six of the principal Dutchmen to meet the Governor. The Staff, also, all came. I again secured my ladies, and, having foreseen that there would be a great deal of company, I had a sly provision of fiddlers ready to give Mrs Blake an impromptu ball. The ball, being unexpected, went off charmingly. Mr Barnard set Mrs Blake a-going, and Sir George had his little lassie again to flirt with. I believe this is the last party we shall ever have in this house. There has been much shabby manoeuvring going forward which has now explained itself, but I trust that temperance, silence, and proper dignity, never asserted until the moment is ripe, will put all things to rights in a little time.

Duminy encouraged English officers to join Lodge de Goede Hoop and many did. At the St John's day festival, in the presence of Craig, all the senior British officers who were Masons were made honorary members. The Grand Registrar of England was impressed, and wrote that 'the Dutch Lodges received the English brethren with open arms and satisfaction.' But at the next term of election in the lodge Duminy professed ill heath, refused to accept the office of Master and resigned.

The next Master, J. Zorn, recognised Truter's natural talent and presence and made him orator. This is unusual as this position is usually given to a very experienced Brother; the orator is the one called upon to present the longest and most complex rituals. Furthermore, you were not automatically made a member nor given office simply because you were initiated in the lodge – you had to first demonstrate your worthiness and only after some time were you invited. Truter was clearly special and he drew many new members to the lodge. Among these he and his old friend Christoffel Brand bullied Christoffel's son, Johannes Hendricus, into joining.

British regiments called regularly at the Cape with many staying for some time. Some of these had travelling warrants and wanted to meet and Lodge de Goede Hoop was anxious to assist, but were in such a muddle themselves they did not know how to handle it. This led to impatience and some of the visiting Masons formed irregular lodges, which led to de Goede Hoop giving permission 'to assemble and exercise the Royal Art , but not to hold receptions or make proselytes until they shall have obtained a constitution.' Another Dutch lodge was also trying to get going: Lodge de Goede Verwagting.

An English lodge was also formed at the time, but with a curious story. Richard Blake arrived at the Cape as private secretary to Governor Sir George Yonge. In England, Blake had played a part in forming the Royal York Lodge No 562 in Bristol in 1789 and became its Master in 1791. The lodge closed down within a short time, 'ruined by extravagance', and its furniture seized and sold. However, Blake brought its minute book and warrant with him to Cape Town. Getting wind of the fact that Africa No. 1 had applied for a warrant, he quickly formed a new lodge with his lapsed warrant which he also called Royal York Lodge. It started working on 24 June 1800 and must have been very successful because the following month Blake bought de Geode Hoop's property in Plein Street for £1 125. When the lodge ceased to exist a few years later Lodge de Goede Trouw took over the building for £1 075; a third of this amount is still owing to this day.

Although there was a degree of rivalry between the lodges, they worked closely as indicated in these minutes: 'She (De Goede Trouw) shall be proposed as a Lawful Lodge by the mother lodge (De Goede Hoop) to the respectable English lodge the Royal York.' They regularly visited each other and traded candidates such as Thomas Rowles who was initiated in the Royal York Lodge and took his other degrees in de Goede Hoop. Blake then applied to Grand Lodge to be appointed as Provincial Grand Master for South Africa; this was agreed to on 13 May 1801. This is puzzling as they had just approved a warrant for their first lodge, Lodge No.

1 at the Cape of Good Hope (Africa Lodge No. 1) and had not yet received their first returns. This, however, resolved itself as Blake left South Africa a few weeks later.

It was during this period of flux that Truter became Master of Lodge de Goede Hoop. Although he was young, he quickly proved himself as attested by this minute: 'the lodge progressed so well during his Mastership that more suitable accommodation was required.' In 1794 it had bought the lodge building and society rooms it had been renting in Plein Street where Barclays Bank stood for many years. The deal was scarcely concluded before Truter decided that it was inadequate for their needs.

The greatness of any man must be dependent on the breadth of his vision and his drive to bring it to fruition. John Truter certainly had a vision for Freemasonry and the will and ability to create it. He saw it as a social force and he engendered a dignity and a pride in the order. He had no qualms about inviting the most senior men to the lodge, including HRH Prince Willem Fredrick Hendrik of the Netherlands. As testimony to his work, there can be few lodges in the world that can boast three presidents, four Governors and a prime minister as members.

When the Garden Domberg came on to the market Truter did not let the grass grow under his feet and sent Thibault to inspect it. A sale was concluded within a few weeks at about £1 400. Truter envisioned a structure that would match his vision for Freemasonry, which at first he was unable to communicate to Thibault and Anton Anreith. The deadlines he gave them were also very short so they initially worked with ideas rather than detailed drawings.

'What do you think?' asked Thibault, peering over Truter's shoulder as the Master inspected the drawings.

'It's good.'

Thibault looked hurt, 'They're great! What do you mean good?'

'Let's look at what you brought,' said Truter, turning to Anreith.

As Anreith unrolled his drawings littered with blots and scratches, Thibault explained the sculptures to Truter. 'They're very good. Look, this statue is Silence, a heroic figure cautioning us not to be loose with our tongues, and this statue of a mother and child represents Grief.'

'We're getting there,' said Truter. Seeing their disappointment, he added, 'No, it's wonderful. But perhaps a little more presence? Have you shown Schutte?'

'Yes,' nodded Thibault. 'Six thousand pounds.'

Truter was quiet for a while, his years as an advocate helping him conceal his shock. Then with a wave of his hand he declared, 'We'll go ahead.'

Truter, being a good manager, left the building work of the new lodge to Thibault and Schutte, his contractor. He visited the site occasionally, but only interfered when there were rumblings about money. The foundation stone was laid a few days later than planned in the presence of Governor Craig and a number of dignitaries. After this, work proceeded with the normal hitches and delays; finances were uppermost in Truter's mind. He increased the membership capacity to thirty-six and these berths were taken up in no time. He also added facilities to make the club more desirable. To add to his worries was news that the British were handing the Cape back to Holland, now the Batavian Republic. Both the Masons and the burghers were nervous of the arrival of the new administration under Baron Abraham de Mist of Uitenhage.

Truter had tried his best to fix the lodge, but he lacked the experience of Masonic practices elsewhere. De Mist was sure to have something to say about it. There was also a revolution taking place in English Freemasonry and its effect was rippling throughout world Freemasonry. One faction, the Moderns, saw Freemasonry in a strict and orthodox way; the other, the Antients, had a more casual approach. Duminy had led Cape Masonry on the Antients' road, while the Dutch were going the other way.

De Mist finally arrived in 1803 and his first job was to consecrate the new lodge building. He declared that it was 'difficult to find another Lodge building in Europe to equal it.' On that occasion he also restored to Lodge de Goede Hoop its original charter with an endorsement that it would be regarded as reinstated as from 1 November 1772. All the brethren in the Colony were invited and were asked to wear black with three-cornered hats. They would meet at two p.m. at Lodge de Goede Trouw and march in procession to the new building. There were at least five meetings during that week at which ten brethren were initiated and four raised through their third degree. At the first meeting held in the new temple, F. A. Duminy, the eighteen-year-old son of Chevalier Duminy, was initiated as a lewis.

De Mist appointed Janssens as the Governor and generally set about remoulding the administration of the Cape. T. R. H. Davenport writes in *South Africa: A Modern History* that these 'two rulers were representatives of the best in revolutionary thought. They were tolerant and allowed all but the senior Orange officials to retain their posts. They again made Dutch the sole official language. They also set about the overhaul of central and local governmental institutions with conviction.' De Mist was not only a

Commissary General of the Batavian Republic, but Deputy Grand Master National of Dutch Freemasonry and he came armed with letters patent to investigate Masonic affairs in the Colony.

De Mist had a lot to do with Truter on a Masonic as well as a governmental level and appeared to admire him. In one of his reports he refers to Truter as 'estimable and learned'. Another said, 'where legal advice and the most patriotic disinterested opinions are required, Mr Truter never fails to give an assistance that may be relied upon for judicial ability and clearness.' Elsewhere Janssens referred to him as his 'able and virtuous friend'. Later in the same year de Mist appointed Truter secretary to the Governor's Council. He was also confident that he could trust Truter to lead Freemasonry in the Cape and appointed him Deputy Grand Master National over all the Lodges in the Batavian colony at the south point of Africa and invested him with his own apron. As soon as de Mist returned to Europe he ratified the arrangements with the Grand East of the Batavian Republic, the new name for the Grand Lodge of the United Netherlands.

With everything now regularised and the faults of the past rectified, Truter stepped down as Master as his day job was becoming more demanding. But the British returned and took the Cape in 1806 and Truter decided he had had enough of government and set up practise as an advocate. He received briefs from the new administrators, including as a member of a commission to investigate a wheat shortage. And in 1809 he returned to government when appointed fiscal. He was not a revolutionary, but a man with a clear view of what was right and good. When he took the post he demanded a flat annual salary of 10 000 rixdollars rather than the 5 200 rixdollars and a third of the fines imposed as he did not believe this was conducive to good legal practice. The thoroughness and clarity he brought to the position was recognised with his elevation to chief justice in 1812, a position he held until retirement in 1827. While chief justice he was instrumental in earmarking the Old Slave Lodge as the site for the new court building and the home of justice in the Cape.

At the consecration of the court he said, 'Everything is precarious the moment we lose sight of justice.' To the advocates he said, 'Do unto others as you would they should do unto you.' To the fiscal, 'May not only the wicked find you continually armed with the rod of justice, but the innocent always consider you as their undaunted defender.' And to the judges he remarked, 'It is not enough for a judge to possess legal knowledge and be gifted with prudence and discretion, but talent and prudence are insufficient if not animated with the most upright intentions to do that which is just.'

In the lodge, Truter was again elected Master in June 1806, but only stayed in the chair for a year before being succeeded by Abraham de Smit. In the middle of de Smit's term something – and the minutes are silent on what exactly – went badly wrong and Truter was persuaded to return with 'full judicial and legislative powers' to sort out the problem, which he did by drafting a set of by-laws which were adopted.

While Master during the second British occupation, he had to deal with another restless wind blowing through Freemasonry.

'We're losing too many English candidates,' said Neethling. 'The 38th Regiment arrived in town and their men are going elsewhere for their initiations and it's killing us.'

'Certainly not the British lodge? They're just about dead?'

'There are military lodges in many regiments, you know,' added van Breda.

'Why don't we all join the British lodge and vote them out?' quipped someone.

'Look, only John and one or two others can perform a decent English working,' observed van Breda. 'I can't blame them for not wanting to join us. It's not only the ritual, but they don't understand us. Not even our jokes.'

'We need to acknowledge that one is only really comfortable in one's own language,' said Truter. 'I suggest that we submit a petition to the Grand Lodge of England to sign it as petitioning members. We'll work in English. It'll be a simple matter to adopt a set of bylaws that bind the new lodge to us.'

Truter was also intimately involved in another first for Freemasonry in South Africa. His family and the Brands, including Grandpa Christoffel, often picnicked together because their children got on well. They agreed to meet at Camps Bay beach and let it be known that they would welcome other Masonic families to join them. It was a beautiful, clear day and Johannes Neethling and Egbertus Bergh and their families took up the offer.

The women set up blankets in the shadow of the rocks, which was extended by a tent the men rigged out of an old sail. There were three huge brass *balies* (jam pots) on the fire with sea water heating up. The ladies paddled in the shallows collecting cockles, periwinkles and what oysters they could find. A bucket of mussels which the boys had collected earlier in the morning had been purged a few times in fresh water and were now lying in water mixed with mielie meal to fatten them. The men smoked their pipes and watched the wine cool in the natural pools while making sure that the rock lobsters that the boys caught did not escape.

At midday, the shellfish went into the pots with celery and seaweed and were eaten as they floated to the top. Then the still flick-ing lobsters went into the pot and when done were split, drenched in butter and served with salads. After lunch the women relaxed against the rocks while the boys, stripped to their breeches, lay on the rocks teasing the blossoming Hanna who had her dress pulled up to her knees as she paddled in the shallow water. The men went for a walk.

'What will young Christoffel be doing next year?' Truter asked.

'I'd like him to study overseas,' replied Johannes. 'But I can't afford the cost.'

'I think we all feel there's a need to help with education,' observed Truter. 'I thought we should establish our own school, but it would take time.'

'Why don't we start an education fund in the lodge; raise money to help all our young people?' suggested Bergh.

'These things only work off a big base,' added Truter. 'We must bring in all the lodges, business, even the Government.'

'Then we'll have to offer them our facilities.'

'John, you're the senior Past Master. Will you talk to the others?' enquired Neethling. 'Come to think of it, you're also the best placed in Government as well. We should also encourage the authorities to establish a proper high school and one day even a university.'

Louis Michel Thibault.

Chapter 5
Louis Michel Thibault

Louis Michel Thibault's life changed with Lodge de Goede Hoop's new building. He could remember the start of it as if it were the day before. They were sitting in John Truter's dining room, the yellowwood table gleaming as it always did. But it was the chandelier that focused their attention on a rolled-out drawing. Cloete's son was, if anything, making better wines than his father did at Klein Constantia, but half-filled glasses of it remained neglected as the three men concentrated on the papers before them. There was a palpable feeling of excitement in the air.

'This is our site,' said Thibault, flattening out the paper and anchoring it with wine glasses. 'It stretches up from Stahl Plein towards the mountain, but looks towards the sea. It's got such potential.'

'Show me the well where we stood yesterday,' said Truter, peering to orientate himself.

'We were here, then we walked this way. You remember where I wanted to put the temple?'

'Tell me about the building. It's got to be special, better than anything else in Cape Town.'

'*Mais oui!* I thought we could have a temple a little bigger than the one in Plein Street.'

'Plein Street! Did you say Plein Street? Don't even think Plein Street. We did not sell that little shed to Blake only to build another,' hissed Truter. 'Listen, *mon ami*, it will be the best building you ever built. When you worked on Versailles—'

'Petit Trianon,' corrected Thibault.

'Yes, yes ... You did not say to King Louis, "we'll make it a little like your grandfather's".'

'Gabriel was the architect; I only helped a little,' Thibault again corrected. 'What about the money? It'll cost more than we have from Blake.'

'Leave the money to me, forget about Blake, we're going to build a monument to Freemasonry that will live forever,' said Truter, putting his arm around Thibault's shoulder. 'In three hundred years' time people will wonder at what we did today. Men will want to join us in our mighty work because of this building. We must remain the best and this building must show that we are.'

'Why am I here?' murmured Anreith.

They both looked round at him.

'You, my friend, are going to make this a very special building. We'll have full-size statues lining the walls. I want a separate temple for the Master's degree, and one for the other orders. The main temple must hold two hundred or more, but must not look silly if there are only a few of us.'

'Well, I don't know how I will do that,' muttered Anreith, even more bewildered.

'You two go off now and work out how and let's meet tomorrow,' said Truter.

'Tomorrow! I'll need a month,' squealed Thibault, looking towards the heavens. '*Mon dieu!*'

'No. A week is all I've got.'

'I'll try; who knows?' said Thibault with a Gallic shrug. Then guiding Anreith out like a man in a trance, he added, '*Allons-y, mon ami.*'

———•———

Thibault was born in 1750 in Picquigny, a small town on the Somme River. We know very little of his early life, but he must have been strongly affected by the architecture of the region. There is a fine old church in his home town and he probably played in the Roman ruins, which must have fired his imagination.

The ruins were his special place, which he told nobody about since he found it a week before. Henri had his house and Pierre claimed another spot and they met in the courtyard of the most complete villa, which was their clubhouse.

'Louis, where are you? Maman says you'd better come home now. You don't want her to come and find you,' his little sister shouted at the top of her voice. 'Louis, where are you?'

He could see her through the crack. When her back was turned he slipped out of his hiding place and pushed a log across the gap before following her.

'I'm coming, I'm coming,' he said, stuffing his latest drawing in his shirt.

'I knew you were here. You know you're not allowed to play in the ruins.'

'I was visiting Pierre when I heard you,' he lied.

'No you weren't. He hasn't seen you since school,' she chirped.

They walked the rest of the way in silence and when he entered the house, his mother demanded, 'Where have you been, Louis?

I hope not those Roman ruins. They'll fall down and kill you and that's before your confirmation on Sunday. Come and wash your hands, papa is back from *boules* and waiting in the lounge.'

He washed his hands in a bucket and as he dried them on his pants he walked through to the lounge. '*Allo*, papa.'

His father put out an arm and gave him a hug. 'We must talk about your future.'

Thibault's father, browned from working in the vineyards, was a little man, not much taller than himself – and he was small for his age.

'Papa, can I not work with you?'

'Nah! Picquigny is too small for you,' he replied sadly. 'Your teacher, Pastor Louverin, tells me you draw very well. And you look at problems differently from the other boys. Your mother always thought you could be an artist.'

'I like drawing.'

'He also told me your mathematics was good while I was beating him at *boules* this evening. It's your confirmation on Sunday and we're going up to Amiens. He has heard that King Louis has opened an Academy for Science that also teaches art. He wants you to study there.'

'But will they let me in?' Louis asked earnestly.

'He has the Monsignor's ear. He was once the confessor to Madam Pompadour when she was married to Lenormand d'Etoiles before King Louis swept her off her feet,' his father said excitedly.

The smell of cooking pervaded the house and their conversation was broken by a call to dinner in the kitchen. Rich onion soup was bubbling in a huge marmite hanging in the hearth over the fire and the iron door of the oven was closed, but could not contain the aroma of the cassoulet. The hearth was festooned with chains of garlic and onions; copper pots glowed in the firelight. Most of the ground floor was taken up with the kitchen, which was also the dining room and workroom. His mother and sisters had laid the L-shaped scrubbed oak table and Louis loved the moment when the family sat down together to give thanks for the food and catch up with their respective days.

After dinner Louis went to his corner on the first floor and got out his drawings of the room in the Roman ruins. What must it have been like then? Pieces of the mosaic floor were still in place; a stern Roman lady looked back at him. The frescos on the wall were still clear where the damp had not peeled them: a cat with a mouse in its mouth, a brace of wild ducks hanging above a stove and many more; he wanted to piece them together before he showed Henri and Pierre. He loved the bold sweep of the vaulting and the thick walls.

It was still dark when the carriage arrived. His parents were shuffling the children in some sort of order so as not to forget one of them. He and his friends Henri and Pierre were pushing and punching one another, which only stopped with a slap on the back of the head from his father. The ladies had packed food and finally they were off, the three boys sitting on the back, feet dangling over the edge. It took a little over two hours to cover the thirteen kilometres to Amiens. The road ran along the Somme River and past farmlands and hamlets. There was a buzz of excitement every time there was a break in the trees and the cathedral could be seen in the distance.

The cathedral at Amiens mesmerised him. The interior was dark and he could see very little until his eyes got used to the gloom. The space was dominated by the columns rising into the dark recesses of the vaults like straight vines, all in logical procession, their rhythms and beat marching up to the altar. Pastor Louverin shepherded them to their seats in the front of the pulpit, just below the crossing, and Louis sat between Henri and Pierre. He had heard of the *Beau Dieu of Amiens*, which separated the great western doors and which Pastor Louverin had said was 'a stately and noble statue' of Christ. *The Bible of Amiens* was a wonder of carved woodwork in the choir stalls, which grasped his attention and soared into the volume of the interior like the branches of a huge tree.

They were nervous as the great organ, which had been rumbling in the background, struck up. Looking back they could see brass crosses moving forward in the gloom followed by a green umbrella, then the choir came into view, then the servers and the Bishop followed by others, including Pastor Louverin. They all wore gold-on-white raiment and the sounds engulfed the mighty space, reverberating to its furthest corners. The choir sang and the men in white read from the Bible, spoke and prayed. It all swirled around his head and he was swallowed up in the imagery of the carvings and the building. At some point he was shuffled between his friends to the kneeling rail and he remembered the Bishop's hand on his head, but was more intrigued by a little carved angel under the pulpit.

Then it was all over; they were in the blinding sunlight. His mother and the other women had commandeered a table and benches and were laying out food. Papa was in deep conversation with the Bishop who did not look nearly so regal without his finery. They were nodding a lot, arms waving about. Everyone was hugging and kissing and shaking hands, but Louis wanted to spend more time looking at the rhythmical detail of the building's architecture.

Pastor Louverin was good as his word. Thibault, now twenty years old, did not know all the strings he had to pull, but he was at last bouncing along by coach on his way to Paris. Many were the nights that he had given up hope of studying in Paris as he passed his years working in the vineyards and for builders, architects and artists in Amiens.

Paris was bewildering, beyond imagining, when Thibault arrived in 1770. The carriage stopped on the south bank of the Seine, near Île de la Cité at the Quai de Montebello. It was good to be out of the rattletrap and to be able to stretch his legs. Driving into Paris, discovering one mighty building after the other, for the last few hours had made him giddy.. And now he was in front of Nôtre Dame Cathedral, which instantly entranced him. He only recovered from his reverie when his bag was thrown from the top of the carriage.

'Go down Saint Michel,' offered the coachman. 'Three streets down you'll find Rue des Écoles. There are thousands of students down there. If you find a sober one ask him for the Royal Academy of Science.'

'Thanks,' muttered Thibault, checking in his bag to see that his precious drawings were not damaged.

He found the academy with a little assistance from a student, who was perfectly sober. Finding A. J. Gabriel was more difficult. The Director was not in his office, but he was eventually tracked down to a large studio full of desks with students everywhere.

'Harumph,' coughed Thibault.

'Yes?' said the great man, carrying on studying a drawing in his hand. Then recognition. 'Ah! The new student. You've got some drawings to show me?'

Some of the students gathered round, a smile here and there

warned him that this was a little fun at the country bumpkin's expense. Even the Director was ready for a laugh as Thibault slid his portfolio from his bag. They can unroll the drawings themselves, he thought, handing the roll to Gabriel. With a degree of reverence, probably to heighten the mirth, Gabriel unrolled them, weighing down the edges with a collection of bits of machinery used as paper weights. But quickly the smiles changed from mirth to genuine appreciation.

'Where's this?' enquired Gabriel.

'Our little church in Picquigny.'

'This one I know – the Beau Dieu of Amiens,' said Gabriel. 'These?'

'The Roman ruins near my home.'

'Come with me,' instructed Gabriel. Turning to the class he said, 'You lot get on with your work.'

He turned on his heel and walked back to his office. Thibault grabbed his drawings, rolling them as he battled to keep pace.

'Sit. Your drawings are good! Very good. The students usually have a little fun at the efforts of potential students, some are really awful, but we teach them,' said the Director, pacing, hands behind his back. Then he launched into his speech, which he had delivered to so many students. 'King Louis, the Sun King, founded this Academy, some say, in imitation of the English Royal Society. I think we have Madam Pompadour to thank, a grand old lady, she gave me your name. You have friends in high places.'

'I did not meet her,' said Thibault, trying to play down any arrogance. 'Pastor Louverin spoke to...'

'No matter. It was sad for us when she died as she always gave us her support, thank the Lord. The Sun King still shone on us until he died two months ago. His grandson, King Louis XV, is continuing with the Academy even though he has little interest in us. He seems to spend all his time chasing women.'

Thibault held his silence. To think such thoughts was dangerous, let alone to say them to a new student.

'A new architectural base has been laid here in Paris by le Vau and Mansard. We're moving away from Baroque toward neo-classicism. We at this academy are changing public taste to a plainer form of architecture that is turning its back on decorative shells with fruit and vegetables filling every available wall. Adam, Soufflot, even Thomas Jefferson the President-architect, are doing plainer work. The church of les Invalides has just been completed, the Panthéon is nearing completion. Tiepolo, Fraganard and David are the great painters of the day, but you can still see the works of Bernini, Rembrandt, Rubens and other Renaissance greats everywhere. The world of science has been set alight with James Watt's steam engine. I'll give you a list of the buildings I want you to visit and I'll expect a drawing of each. I also want you to see the art in the city. I want a sketch every week of a great work. I want your eyes to be your teacher. You will work in the studio five days a week, six hours a day; you will work with a small team. Speak to the porter; he'll find a place for you to stay.'

Paris became the centre of the world for young Thibault, tramping the streets for many hours after work and during weekends. Coming home late by the newly installed oil street lights, he wondered when he would find time to relax. At first, being in the studio was hell. He did not even have a desk, but was given full-size details to draw on brown paper on the floor. Most of his time he spent grinding colours while preparing linen and parchment. That soon stopped when he won his first student competition for *A Gateway to a Commercial Town*. By the time he had won his second competition two months later for *An Altar for the Principal Chapel in a Circular Building*, everyone wanted to work with him. Even Gabriel.

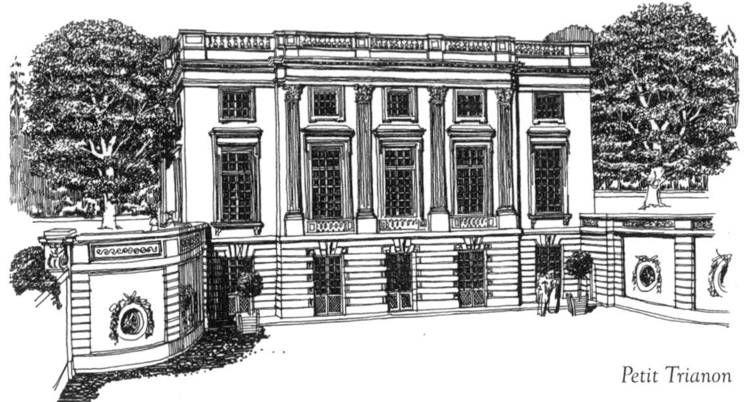

Petit Trianon

Gabriel had been commissioned to design Petit Trianon, a small palace in the grounds of Versailles. It was to be the King's gift to his Lady, Madame du Barry. Gabriel needed a gopher with some talent and took Thibault to the site with him. He learned much from Gabriel on their long carriage rides on which the great man spoke to him. No response was needed and Louis tried to remember and take in all the philosophies and anecdotes about clients and builders. One glance at Koopmans de Wet House in Cape Town will confirm that the lessons learned here never left Thibault.

Louis XV was succeeded by Louis XVI, whom H. G. Wells described as 'a dull well meaning man, an excellent shot and amateur locksmith of some ingenuity.' These are not perhaps the qualifications one would look for in a king, but as a patron of the academy he devoted much of his time to it and its students. He kept Gabriel on as its director. He would have been hard-pressed to dismiss him as his wife Marie Antoinette had fallen in love with Petit Trianon.

On 21 September 1776, Thibault, as one of the academy's brighter students, had the honour of presenting the King with a model he had made in terracotta of a French Order of Architecture, which he had designed. This 3' 6"-high model consisted of three columns arranged in plan on an equilateral triangle. The base, shaft and capital were enriched with an abundance of floral decorations, the whole being very original and pleasing. The drawing of this architectural motif is still preserved at the Cape in the Kolbe collection. To the drawing Thibault added the following inscription recalling this memorable event in his life as a student: 'Plan of a French Order designed by myself and a French Engineer in 1774 and presented to the King on 21 September 1776. The model was made by me in terracotta. I was then in Paris holding position of premier student at the Royal Academy of Architecture.'

From this we can deduce a number of things about Thibault. First, he was no shrinking violet. He was the premier student at the academy, or thought he was, and he was not shy for everyone to know it. Indeed, he was going to make sure that as many people as possible knew it. In an architect this is acceptable, if not mandatory. Second, he was clearly a man of talent. A talentless architect does not win competitions and prepare designs of sufficient quality to present to the King. And thirdly, he had great love of architecture.

All of this makes it difficult to explain why, soon after he had completed his studies, he gave it all up to join the army – the Corps des Ponts et Chaussé where Charles Daniel de Meuron sent him to study military engineering in 1781. Was it a lack of work? Hardly.

Even though France was on a rollercoaster downhill it did not stop Marie Antoinette from spending money. Was he looking for a safe sinecure in the protected environment of the army? Did he have romantic notions of the army? This makes little sense as the only war in this period was the American War of Independence. A scandal perhaps? No, because he hardly left Paris. It is most likely that the Renaissance dream of the complete man inspired him to branch out to other disciplines to be like his heroes, Leonardo da Vinci and Michelangelo, who both studied military engineering.

At the age of 31 he commenced studies in that discipline. His regiment was hired by the VOC and he was sent to the Cape in 1783. He left Europe as a private, but was soon promoted to lieutenant, then captain. He was obviously someone people noticed. Professor Fransen described him as 'a typical Frenchman, small of stature with a volatile and aggressive temperament.' He was not afraid to make a stand on something he believed in. This often got him into trouble with the authorities. He had an undeniable talent and intelligence as well as great charm to help overcome the trouble his tactlessness often caused him.

⪢•⪡

'Send Captain Thibault in,' van Plettenberg called through the open door.

The pimply young secretary swung his head toward the door and carried on with what he was doing.

'Something should be done about this dismal old castle,' thought Thibault, unable to stop thinking like an architect.

Governor van Plettenberg was a smallish, dapper man, with white hair raked back into a tight ponytail. He made a slight effort to stand as he beckoned Thibault to a chair.

'I understand you're a military engineer.'

'That's correct, sir. How can I help?'

'I want you to map out our defences and work up plans to improve them. Get in touch with François Duminy who's charting the coast.'

Thibault was pleased by the thought of working with Duminy, who had invited him to a society dinner at the lodge. There he found himself sitting between Johanna Duminy and Elizabeth van Schoor, the beautiful daughter of Evert van Schoor, a Freemason, burgher and councillor in Cape Town. Thibault knew he was being wooed by Duminy into joining the lodge.

Soon afterwards, van Plettenberg was replaced as Governor by an aggressive military man, van der Graaff, and Thibault was in great demand. He knew that his post at the Cape was temporary and he could be sent anywhere in the world at the whim of his superiors. That was the last thing he wanted, especially since his relationship with Elizabeth started to show real promise. The itch for design also started to creep into his soul. The architecture of the Cape had a sort of muddled charm. There was so much ground available and very little need for multi-storey buildings. Some builders had tried to import the multi-storey gables of the cities of the lowlands, but with little success. The Cape's most notable architectural feature was the entrance to the Castle, but this was merely a copy of a gateway to a small provincial town. But he had little leeway for expression as his work was mainly limited to warehouses, maintenance and the odd defence structure.

These led to him resigning from the VOC in 1785 and marrying Elizabeth on 2 April 1786. But he kept an interest in the military and the following year was put in charge of the Military Academy for Artillery Cadets. There was no shortage of work for a man of his talents and he was offered a number of public appointments, but he soon resumed his former profession as an architect and built up a flourishing practice. The VOC was not going to let him go that easily and persuaded him to take the post of superintendent of its buildings, which he accepted, but on a fairly loose rein because we know he started to work on many private contracts such as Groot Constantia, completed in 1789, the Kat Balcony (1790), and Tokai, where he for the first time experimented with a rectangular pediment.

When exactly Thibault became a Freemason we do not know. It was probably soon after he arrived in 1783, but there are no records for the two years before Lodge de Goede Hoop closed down in 1785. Various experts suggest he may have joined on the high seas or perhaps before he left Europe; some even suggest he might have left France because of Louis XVI's condemnation of Masonry. What we do know is that on 24 June 1794, when Lodge de Goede Hoop was re-established, his name was listed among the founders, seven of whom had been either members or had taken degrees in the former lodge. To be listed among the new founders, he must have been a man of some Masonic substance. Three years later he proposed his old friend Thomas Anrit, sometimes called Anton Anrieth, into the lodge.

When the Cape fell to the British in 1795, Thibault still held his post as Chief Military Engineer. It was in this capacity that he signed the inventory of the buildings, fortifications and estates for the handover to the new administration. This document reads as follows:

Inventory of such companies, buildings, fortifications and estates etc, as were existent at the surrender of the Cape of Good Hope to the arms of his Brittanic Majesty and at present according to capitulation and by order of the undersigned Commissary of this Government are delivered by the Major of the Artillery, George Coenraad Kuchler and the Captain of Engineers, Louis Michel Thibault, for a receipt to the Captain of the Engineers, Bridges and said lieutenant of the said Engineers, Elphinstone, commissioned for this purpose by the Commanding officers of his said Majesty.

These must have been confusing times for Thibault. He was French and traditionally an enemy of England, but had also been involved in some sensitive military matters. Whereas the British left most officials in their posts, he felt pressure. He had grown to love the Cape, however, writing, 'I love this Colony and have lived here for seventeen years and decided to remain here with my family, live in an honourable manner and make myself useful during the years that remain for me to work.' So, as his private practice was growing, he decided to stay and focus on it. He resigned and at first refused to have anything to do with the new occupiers.

An old house on Strand Street was bought by Koopmans de Wet and Thibault was engaged to rebuild it. He added a floor and a new facade on classical lines reminiscent of Petit Trianon. You can see the derivation and innovation, which Pearse describes:

The facade is [also] divided vertically by four pilasters carrying a well-designed cornice and pediment. Its charm lies in the quiet dignity and proportion of the whole.

The door [where Thibault broke away for a bit of fun] is framed in by fluted pilasters and an entablature, a free rendering of the Doric order. The fan light has radiating bars, an unusual type and is fitted with a lantern [an invention of Thibault's so that the lantern was internally housed, but lit the pavement externally].

Koopmans de Wet House

Thibault's value was known to the British, however. General Craig offered him 100 guineas for the maps he had compiled for the VOC and the post of Royal Geographical Engineer for the Colony. He politely declined. In spite of the rebuff, or perhaps because of it, a cordial relationship developed between the two. It was a major stand for Thibault to take when the amount offered represented several months of earnings and Thibault was short of funds. But it was admired by Craig and his successors, Lord Macartney and General Dundas. Of them, Thibault writes, 'I have always been honoured by the protection of these gentlemen.' He continues that Dundas proposed that 'as architect I should take charge and superintend repairs to the military buildings of the garrison which had been completely ignored for 5 years. And having suffered considerably by the loss of my profession, I accepted.'

Thibault's employment by the British was a very comfortable and rewarding one until the new Governor, George Yonge, arrived. The trouble began when the architect invited Yonge's aide-de-camp, Lieutenant Colonel Cockburn, to view his studio. He paid little attention to his designs and drawings, but a great deal of interest in his maps. A few days later he was invited to meet Yonge, who asked him to show him the maps. The official then refused to hand them back. At first, the Governor simply was unavailable to him when he presented himself at the Castle every day for three weeks. Yonge sent him a message that he would send for him when he saw fit. He then simply confiscated the maps, stating that he felt that 'it was contrary to the security of the Cape for the best plans to be in the hands of a former official and artillery training officer of the Dutch East India Company.'

Thibault's old friend, General Dundas, interceded by writing to his friend William Huskisson, Colonial Agent in London, in a famous letter dated 15 October 1800. Two excerpts are of interest:

> The plans which Sir George Yonge wished to possess have been until now considered the property of Thibault, and as they are very well drawn Sir James Craig offered him one hundred guineas for one of them, which he refused. On my advice permit poor Thibault to keep his plans which can do no more harm to the security of the Colony than a wisp of straw.

In the same letter, Dundas writes 'As an engineer officer his capabilities are mediocre but can be usefully employed in architecture, which has been his principal study and in which he has given proof of much taste.'

His maps were returned to him with an insulting letter forbidding him to make further maps without permission and that permission would not be granted. Yonge was high-handed with everyone and was resented by all, particularly when he closed the gates of the Company Gardens to the public and kept them for himself. Six months later, on 20 April 1801, Yonge was relieved of his office to be replaced by Dundas until the Cape was handed back to the Dutch.

When the Garden Domberg came up for sale, Thibault and Anreith were given very little time by Truter to come up with the concept and plans for the lodge buildings and sculptures. What Truter did say was that he wanted the finest lodge building in the world, irrespective of cost. The pair hardly slept as they brainstormed ideas for a week. When they met with Truter at the end of the week he accepted their proposals in principle. Thibault's designs were placed before the lodge some time in September or October 1800 and the elevations and sections survive to this day and hang in the vestibule.

In characteristic fashion, Truter immediately got on with the planning and Thibault and Anrieth were appointed architect and sculptor. We do not know where Lodge de Goede Hoop met for the next twenty-one months – perhaps they shared with Royal York or used the farmhouse on their new site. A construction price was received from Herman Schutte to the amount of £6 000 and contracts were resolved by November and work was started immediately. In December 1800 the lodge took a decision to lay the foundation stone 'with full Masonic honours' on 5 February 1801. The ceremony actually took place a few days later.

Schutte was a very good builder but very poor at costing and he was continually in financial trouble. The result was an overrun of £800. There were no specific items which seemed to have caused the over expenditure, but from the tenor of the minutes it appears there was a miscalculation by Schutte and that the building took almost two years to build, which, even then, was excessively long and added to costs. Other factors that could have contributed was that the Cape had been making bricks since 1654 and burning lime since 1665 (it is interesting to note that the lime kiln at Mowbray was still working until comparatively recently), but at this particular time Mantzel records that 'there was no one in town burning bricks or lime.' These now had to be imported from Holland as well as the glass, face-bricks and paving slabs, which must have created a planning nightmare.

The success of the Lodge de Goede Hoop building brought Thibault, Schutte and Anreith renown; especially Thibault. He was immediately commissioned to build two Drosdys: one in Graaff-Reinet and the other in Tulbach, which were started in 1804. Sadly the one in Tulbach has been demolished, but the one in Graaff-Reinet has been converted into a wonderful hotel. Thibault was very unhappy with the latter as it was too far away for him to supervise properly and the local builders took liberties with his designs.

In late 1805 Thibault was commissioned to redesign and rework Rust-en-Vreugd. It was originally built in 1777 in the fashionable Buitenkant area of the city by hated and corrupt independent fiscal Willem Cornelis Boers. Pat Hopkins writes in *Ghosts of South Africa*:

It is said to be the most haunted house in Cape Town. Built in the rococo style, it is double-storeyed, with huge rooms and lofty ceilings. Its feature is the portico and woodwork by artist Anton Anreith. 'The house is remarkable for a portico, supported by Corinthian columns of carved teak, and for the enrichment of the front door and first-floor French window,' wrote C. de Bosdari in *Anton Anreith*. 'The front is a double door, reached by a lateral flight of steps – originally they were probably two symmetrical lateral flights – and is framed by teak pilasters, panelled and moulded; the transom is much enriched and the fanlight carved in a markedly baroque design. The richness of transom and fanlight is repeated over the tall French window on the first floor, but the entire frame is now an intricate and ornate piece of carving, reminiscent of the elaborate carving sometimes given to baroque mirrors. This is certainly the finest door at the Cape.' ...

After Boers was recalled it had a number of residents, including Governor Lord Charles Somerset. It is now a museum and houses the Dr William Fehr collection of watercolours and rare prints. Also there are a number of unknown apparitions. There are footsteps, with some people experiencing a tap on the shoulder by a hidden hand. A woman floats between rooms downstairs, and another peers across the city from an upstairs window. By her side is an empty crib.

Thibault was commissioned to beautify the Parade by Governor de Graaff during the Batavian period. He proposed a fountain in the form of a small round Roman temple on the spot where the old gallows mound stood. There are drawings of it and work was started but never completed.

When the British reoccupied the Cape it brought a new round of prosperity; especially from Thibault's point of view. He was commissioned to design every new government building over the next ten years, including conversion of the Old Slave Lodge at the end of the Heerengracht (now Adderly Street) to a new Supreme Court building. This building is almost as old as the Castle and it is clear that Thibault was the only one to be trusted with the work. As J. J. Oberholster, the longest serving member of South Africa's National Monuments Council, states, 'It is a remarkable building. Its history, its architectural merits and its significance make it unique in South Africa.' Thibault brought Anreith onto the team for this hugely symbolic project. The work on the Supreme Court seemed to be an ongoing business as one portion after the next was added.

Thibault weathered the storm of the second British invasion in 1806 better than he did in 1795. No one could deny his talent as an architect and he had been employed by them on a number of projects, but in 1807 they seemed far more interested in his ability as a surveyor, perhaps because of his earlier contretemps with them and his maps. They appointed him Chief Surveyor and whereas he was still busy with the Supreme Court he became more involved in surveying which, according to his wife, led to a decline in his health.

Thibault was still very much involved with the lodge and was still its official architect during this time. There is a minute in 1809 in which Thibault was called upon to draw plans for the new Slave

Quarters under the stoep of the society rooms. It was also about this time that he started working on the banqueting hall for the lodge. On 31 December 1811, Thibault was instructed to prepare designs for a new courtroom in the centre of the Supreme Court building, which was the last piece to be added to complete its development and his last major building. The start was delayed and it was only finally completed and ready for use by 14 January 1815 on which date it was 'dedicated to justice' by Truter.

By the time he reached the age of 60 he had two dreams yet to see fulfilled: the establishment of the Masonic Institution and the building of the society rooms of the lodge. The Masonic Institution was a school for craftsmen established by the Masons. Truter had a passion for education and contributed his own money to the project. It was Thibault who saw the need to develop local craftsmen and it was his project more than anyone else's. He started working on it in 1813, but did not live to see it opened in 1815, the year of his death.

The building of the society rooms had been debated on a number of occasions. In 1810, a vote was taken and defeated 10-9, but ten days later a new vote succeeded 18-3. We have no record of when work on the rooms started, but know that they were opened in 1816. Thibault never saw them completed, but he had finished the designs. Part of the complex was the banqueting hall, which was a large, simple room of magnificent proportions with five long windows on each side. It had such presence that it was chosen and rented from the lodge by the Cape Parliament as its House of Assembly from 1854-1884.

Thibault died on 4 November 1815 (even though the church register records it as 3 November), ten months after he finished the Supreme Court. Although he was only 65 we can deduce that he had not been well for some time before that. In Lady Anne Barnard's letter dated 1807 she refers to him as 'old Thibault'. She was very fond of him and had great respect for him, believing him to be a man of great talent. She referred to his house for the Governor at Papenboom as 'the only building in Africa'. The only portrait of Thibault was executed by her. Another friend, Craig, referred to him as 'poor Thibault'. Neither of these epithets was derogatory and can only be referring to his health. He left his wife and two unmarried daughters in very poor circumstances, a sad reflection on departed merit.

Thibault was South Africa's first architect and he, more than anyone else, helped establish the first recognisable local architectural style that became known as South African Cape Dutch. He was buried by the lodge in a simple tomb, built by Schutte and possibly designed by himself, in the Somerset Road Cemetery. The tomb was later demolished and there is no record of the final resting place of his mortal remains. It sounds like a sad, almost pitiful end to so great a man and of course it is, but we can glory in what he left behind – a celebration in wood and stone of the joy of life.

Chapter 6
Herman Schutte

There was a loud crack like a rifle shot. Herman Schutte looked up at the slate cliff; he was sure it moved. Platneus, Hendrik and Jaintjies were working below.

'Out, out!' he shouted, running for all he was worth.

They were hammering away, prising slabs of slate away with crowbars. Had they not heard it?

'For God's sake, get out of there!'

He could see the sun reflecting off the sweat of their bodies.

'Out, Platneus! Get out!'

Gradually, the top of the cliff started to slide. He was there grabbing at the three men; Jaintjies and Platneus scrambled out of the hole, and with awful clarity he could see Hendrik trip on his own ragged work clothes.

'No!'

He had a hand on Hendrik's shoulder when the cliff came down. The noise was greater than anything he could imagine, Hendrik was a screaming, dust everywhere, filling his lungs. Then the screaming stopped. The numbness in his left side started to abate and waves of pain racked his body before blackness took over. He swam up to the surface of his consciousness. The pain in his arm and head were excruciating, he could hear Platneus and Jaintjies frantically pulling the slabs of slate aside, shouting instructions to one another and calling to the rest of the crew. In and out of consciousness the pain continued, his head was in Platneus's lap, Jaintjies was holding his arm.

'Faster, you bliksem!' yelled Platneus

Then soft velvet black. When he came to he was lying in crisp white sheets, he could sense many people in the room, his head was bound, his arm was numb with a persistent throb, then he was gone again to a time long ago. He was working on the floor as all architectural apprentices did. The master of the studio sketched the building in rough, the senior assistants then working them up on linen and ink. On the floor he drew the details to full size on coarse brown paper with charcoal and chalk. Heinrich, his personal mentor, came up and smudged all over it, pointing out with some degree of satisfaction where he had gone wrong, ordering him to start over again. The scene kept changing; he now had a pair of compasses in his hands, mapping out an arch over the entrance of a fine building. The lights shone behind his right eyelid, he could hear a voice – was it Anreith? – 'He's lost it.' Lost what, what have I lost?

'We'll have to take it off here.'

Was the laudanum playing with his mind? He was getting onto a VOC ship heading for the Cape. He was an architect, not a sculptor, not a builder; what was he doing on this ship? He was 28. There was only one building in Bremen worth a damn: the old Rathaus built in 1612. Inky blackness swallowed him in its bosom, some long time later he swam up to the light. A most beautiful face emerged into his view.

'Just lie still,' said a nurse. 'We could not save your hand.'

Then nothing.

———•———

Schutte is an enigma. Born in Bremen on Christmas Day, 1761, he was apprenticed to an architect in Hanover before entering the services of the Dutch East India Company at fourteen guilders a month. He came to the Cape in 1789, where he was described as a sculptor, architect and builder. On arrival he was sent to work in the quarries on Robben Island as a stone dresser, which could not have impressed him. Though sullen, he became good friends with Anton Anreith, possibly because they were both German, Lutheran and attended church house meetings. Moreover, they were both bachelors trained in the visual arts and exposed to the same architectural background.

Shortly after being discharged from hospital, he sought an appointment with Governor van Plettenberg.

'Come in Schutte, sit down. We're terribly sorry about your accident; it's a miracle you're alive,' said the Governor, ushering him in.

'Hendrik died. What are you doing for him?'

'He was a slave with no family.'

'He was a kind, gentle man.'

'What can we do for you, Schutte? You know that we'll find a job for you.'

'I'm confused at the moment, sir,' shrugged Schutte, holding up his left arm which was still in a sling. 'My thoughts are still in a muddle, but I'd like you to discharge me from Company service.'

'That I can arrange, but it seems unfair to me.'

'I want you to make over Platneus and Jantjies to me.'

'The slaves?'

Schutte nodded, 'I'll free them as soon as I can pay them. And I want you to instruct Thibault, your superintendent of buildings, to give me building work. I promise it'll be well done.'

Schutte, given six months' salary, was able to set up a building company, which was noted for its good work and abominable costings that were usually too low. On site he cut a piratical figure – tall with long blond hair tied back with black ribbon, a patch over one eye (the other lost in the accident on Robben Island) and a black cloak draped over his left arm to hide his missing hand. Platneus and Jantjies worked for him and Thibault directed projects his way, mostly boring repairs and alterations to Company buildings. It was, however, a good learning period; it was not easy to build proper buildings in the Cape as there were no stocks of building materials and almost everything had to be gathered and made.

The stone was mostly unsuitable and acquiring lime for plaster and bricks was a serious challenge. Brass and copper were difficult to obtain locally, and though clay bricks had been made since van Riebeeck's time, they were in short supply. Most of the bricks, known as *klompjes*, were imported. Used as ballast on Company ships, these small, yellow face-bricks weathered to a deep gold. Van Plettenberg's replacement, Governor Cornelis Jacob van der Graaff, did sort out the timber industry, which made the acquisition of hardwood easier.

Thibault and Anreith were given the job of building the new Lutheran Pastorie and Schutte was in the front line for his first big job. Though he came in cheaply, he was surprised that they had budgeted even less. The pair had been after him to join the lodge and Duminy had had a word with him, so they were delighted when he agreed. While he related to the symbolism and ideal of immemorial brotherhood, he still held himself aloof. Nonetheless, he was given the contract, but it nearly ended in financial disaster as very soon even his contingency had been eaten up. At the end of the job there was barely enough to start another one, but he did keep his promise to free Platneus and Jaintjies.

Schutte kept up appearances at the Lutheran church mainly, one suspects, because of Susanne van der Poel, who would keep a place for him. They attended church socials and later were to marry with Anreith as his best man and Thibault making a speech. In June 1800 Truter was again elected to the chair of the lodge and Schutte found himself enjoying his Masonry more as there was a new feeling of buoyancy. While Thibault had fallen out with the new British administration, he prospered as Captain Bridges sent more lucrative work in his direction. Then Thibault appeared at his office door carrying a roll of drawings.

'What brings you to my humble office?' smiled the German, clearing place for his friend on the riempie bench.

Thibault unrolled the drawings and smoothed them over Schutte's papers, 'Truter decided to buy the Garden Domberg.'

'I heard it was for sale. But what happened to "Good morning my good friend. How are you?"'

'Good morning,' blushed Thibault. 'Truter is not a man to let grass grow under his feet and wants more suitable accommodation.'

'But he's just bought the building we're in.'

'Richard Blake with his Royal York Lodge offered to buy it.'

'What will we do in the interim?'

'I don't know. Perhaps rent space from Royal York.'

'Let's start again. Good morning, Louis. How is your darling wife?'

There was a rumour that Thibault was having an affair with Lady Anne Barnard, and now that she was due to go back to England, he was very morose.

'She's fine, thank you, Herman. Can we start now?'

'What have we here?'

'It had better be the best Masonic temple in the world. That's what Truter's expecting.'

'It's certainly big enough!' said Schutte. 'Why's the main lodge room so long and thin?'

'I want it like that. It needs to hold a lot of people, but not look empty when it's not so full.'

Schutte mumbled, 'I see.'

'What will it cost?'

'Give me a couple of days.'

'I'm going to see Truter this afternoon. He'll want to know what it will cost.'

'No, no. I'm not falling for that trap. Tell him to wait.'

'Just an idea, I won't hold you to it.'

'I've heard that before, the first figure in their heads remains there forever, no matter what changes occur. What finishes are you thinking of?'

'Good.'

'What's good? Give me some specifications and a few days.'

'I haven't got either.'

'£6 000.'

'What? You're joking.'

'No time, no specs, £6 000.'

'Thank you. I must go and give the bad news.'

With that Thibault was gone, rolling the plans on the way.

'Damn! Damn!' cursed Schutte, who had vowed never to be

pressured into a costing again.

Susanne came in with a tea tray, 'Where is he?'

'Gone.'

'You gave him an estimate, didn't you? I saw the drawings under his arm, now gone in ten minutes. You promised me you would not let anyone bully you into prices out of thin air.'

'I didn't give him a price, only a rough guess.'

Later that afternoon Thibault returned with Anreith to announce that Truter had accepted the price. The generous man had again been tricked, but he was as excited as his friends who he had worked with well in the past. And he was going to be part of a great creation which Thibault assured him would cost within budget.

'You tell me what I can include and I'll try to work with it,' said Thibault reassuringly. 'We'll work backwards to the cost.'

'What roof?'

'Puddled clay.'

There was a groan from Schutte.

'Flat roofs always leak?' added Anreith.

'Not mine,' said Schutte. 'But it's expensive. Puddled clay or a sort of lime concrete laid on a bed of reeds is not what costs. Keeping it waterproof is. I use two parts broken bricks ground to a powder mixed with four parts gravel of sea shells from the bottom of a lime kiln, two parts mason's lime well mixed, then I run coconut oil into it so that it remains tacky, and then knead it into a dough and beat it with mallet into a 1½-inch layer. Onto that I work...'

'Yes, we know you'll do it right,' said Thibault, wanting to get onto more interesting matters. 'The floors have to be special – marble.'

'£7 000 and six months,' grinned Schutte.

'Listen here, Herman, the cost we're talking about will build twenty lodges.'

'We've no marble here. Perhaps a mixture of grey mountain stone and slate for the main room. I could even lay a tessellated pavement for you like King Solomon's temple. I have some *klompjes* for the steps and stoeps and some *tigglesteentjes* for smaller rooms.'

'We'll need brass for our metalwork. Do you think Truter, our assistant fiscal, can lean on the British to let some through to us?'

'Look, we'll be here all night. Why don't you draw up a finishing schedule for Herman?' suggested Anreith, not realising that Thibault was on a fishing exercise trying to find out what Schutte had stuck away that they could use.

Susanne brought sherry, brandy and wine with a cheese board.

'Aha! Herman you're so lucky having a wife who knows what the inner man needs,' said Anreith, shuffling to help her.

'He wants to start in a month,' said Thibault.

Susanne spun round, 'Now, listen here, we're not starting anything until we've got it all worked out. A contract, dates, costs, plans. But why so soon?'

'Truter thinks the Batavians will be taking over the Cape again and he wants the temple up before then,' replied Thibault.

'Did he tell you that?' demanded Susanne.

'Well, not exactly. He spoke about us having to toe the line from a Masonic point of view. He also spoke about the situation in Europe, that there's no reason France should continue in power in Holland. With them pulling out there's no point in England staying here.'

'That's not the same as saying the Batavians are coming back, nor is it a reason to start before we have all our ducks in a row,' proclaimed Susanne.

Platneus and Jantjies had set up the little fence profiles outside the line of the building so that Schutte could accurately set out the building.

'Noni, Susanne says we're not to start until there's a contract,' muttered Platneus, knocking in nails.

'I have a sort of contract,' mumbled Schutte. 'Thibault showed me the minutes of the committee meeting. It says: "a contract was entered into with Herman Schutte to erect it for £6 000 on his estimate."'

The work went well, as did his jobs at the Castle. Macartney was replaced by Sir George Yonge as Governor and Andrew Barnard played a part in keeping the public works flowing in his direction. He was due to leave any day now with his wife, Lady Anne. He hoped he could get on with the new man. Susanne had not spoken to him for a day or two, but he was optimistic that everything would work out. But he was concerned that there were still discussions about finishes and details. Perhaps she was right for being angry with him. A few days later all the Masons were there: Thibault was explaining, Truter was concentrating hard, Duminy was keenly trying to understand, and there was van Schoor, Burger, de Wet and old Christoffel Brand being helped by Anreith over piles of sand.

When they got to where Schutte was waiting, the builder took Truter's hand, 'Master, I welcome you to my site.'

'I see you've made a valiant start,' complimented Truter. 'You know we'll be laying the foundation stone on 5 February 1801 with full Masonic honours. His Excellency, Major General Dundas, the acting Governor, has accepted the honour of laying it. Admiral

Curtis, Mr Holland, my boss the fiscal van Ryneveld, Mr Secretary Barnard, Count d'Forchincourt, members of the Court of Justice, members of the municipal council, the Masters and wardens of the other lodges will be present.'

'I didn't know His Excellency was opening it for us,' replied Schutte. 'I imagine the stonemasons have all the details for the foundation stone itself.'

Thibault and Anreith gave him a withering stare. I thought as much, Schutte smiled to himself.

'Are the foundations sound?' asked Truter.

Schutte jumped into the trench with a hammer and peg, which scarcely penetrated.

'See,' he proclaimed as Platneus arrived with brandy and glasses. 'Gentlemen, there's a sacred old ceremony still practiced on prestigious buildings in Germany to bless the foundations for centuries to come. First we need to drink to the future. This day we are about to begin a great work. May peace reign within these walls and banish all evil or ill humour. May we work toward the good of mankind, ever remembering the commandment to love one another. Now we all line up on the side of the trench to consecrate these foundations.'

'That is an unusual ceremony,' commented Anreith afterwards.

'That's because I invented it,' laughed Schutte, putting an arm around Platneus. 'We can't have them too sober.'

The laying of the foundation stone was delayed, an embarrassment because it had been advertised in the press. No one could give him the right words for the stone itself: Thibault tried to get the right ranks and decorations of the Governor from Lady Anne Barnard and there was an argument about the Masonic date. Finally Truter wrote out the words for him and Platneus carved them on the stone Schutte was saving for his own grave. In spite of the delays, he was ready on time, but Dundas was unable to attend on the appointed day.

The works were not that difficult, but it did not go as well as planned because news was received that the British were indeed giving the Cape back to the Batavians, which meant that the importation of non-essential goods was virtually impossible. So everything, including *klompjes* bricks, copper, brass, glass and timber, was scarce. Schutte warned the lodge, but they had faith in him as he was buying up old cooking vessels for their metal and offered to demolish old buildings for free to get to their materials. Still he was having trouble keeping up with his programme.

Somehow the building did get completed just before Commissary Abraham de Mist arrived, but many of the sculptural niches were empty as Anreith was battling for materials and could only start work on site after it was waterproofed. In June 1803, Truter led a deputation to see de Mist to ask him to dedicate the new building. Truter, as Master, and de Mist, one of the most senior Freemasons in the world, spent much time discussing the global changes in Freemasonry. All the known brethren in the colony were invited in writing and the rest were invited by way of an advertisement in the *Kaapsche Courant*. They were asked to wear black with three-cornered hats, to meet at 2 p.m. at Lodge de Goede Trouw and march to the new building in procession. There were over 200 brethren there.

Like most Masonic ceremonies, it involved many processions. In ancient tradition the guests were seated, then the brethren paraded in ascending order, in groups, each greeted with standing applause and the peal of the organ. Normally Schutte, as a junior, would have been in early and seated, but as he was nominated to carry the wine, he marched in with Thibault and Anreith behind Truter; de Mist and the wardens were all marshalled behind the director of ceremonies. They sang the opening hymn, the Master opened the lodge and then proceeded to welcome and greet all the visitors. The consecration ceremony was simple with von Manger, the chaplain, marching round the chequered floor swinging a sensor, chanting the age-old incantations, with Truter and de Mist following. The three stood to one side with silver cornucopias.

'With this corn we ask thee, our Great Architect of the Universe, to bless this building to thy use. May honourable men ever find brotherly love within its walls.'

Thibault stepped forward with a silver cornucopia of corn and de Mist took some and spread it on the floor.

'With this wine we ask thee, our Lord, to bless this building to thy use. May honourable men find the wine of relief.'

Truter stepped forward to take the wine from Schutte and pour it onto a tray on the floor.

'With this oil we ask thee, Great Architect of the Universe, to visit this building with thy truth.'

Anreith handed the oil, which was likewise poured on the floor. This done, a nod from the director of ceremonies sent the three back to their seats.

His building looked wonderful, every seat filled with men who were proud to be there, in their black suits, gold jewels twinkling from chains and collars, white aprons fringed with colour. Processions in perfect order moved through its spaces, taking the eye on a focal journey. Thibault may claim ownership, so may Truter, but it was Schutte's building; it was he who lived through its birth, he who knew its walls like his own skin, he who breathed life into its spaces, he who agonised when its bones failed to come together.

Truter made a speech of thanks in which he tried to thank everyone. De Mist then handed out a gold medal to Thibault for his design and a silver to Schutte, but embarrassingly there was no recognition for Anreith.

The lodge got off to a busy start; the first meeting was a stormy affair. First on the agenda was the snub of Anreith.

'There's another weighty matter to discuss,' said Truter, unpacking documents from an envelope. 'The works have considerably overrun budget. We're looking at an extra £800.'

The lodge committee was unhappy and not in a mood to settle easily; they could not understand how the cost had risen as there was no real change to the design. Truter was a judicial man; to him things were either black or white, while Thibault understood the vagaries of the building industry but was embarrassed by it all.

'Look, Schutte has put forward some telling arguments,' said Truter. 'Let me read his claim to you:

1. We have been making bricks here since 1654; they were not marvellous but if you plastered over them they would last for a hundred years. We always imported *klompjes* and *tigglesteentjes* for fireplaces, steps and tiles for floors, but the Company always made commons. The British came and took over and suddenly there was nobody making common bricks and we had to import from Holland. I even tried to make my own bricks, but the English forbid us to cut chaff because it caused erosion, and it was too far to go to find it.

2. Then the lime. Suddenly there were no more shells on the beach to burn, thank the Lord we found deposits

in Mowbray, but it is far and expensive.

3. Brother François Duminy started the timber industry in Plettenberg Bay. The British come and fire him. No timber.

4. And labour; they clamp down on slave-ownership and give them rights.

5. British clamped down on brass and lead because it was a strategic resource. I had to salvage materials.

6. You did not make decisions in time then changed your mind.'

The members were in a difficult position: some vehemently disagreed with paying the overrun; others argued that he was a brother and they could not let him sink. It was left to Truter, who took a pragmatic approach as he had already taken action to increase the lodge's income. He had increased the membership to thirty-six as well as the number of society days. After eighteen months, we read in the minutes of January 1804, 'the building of the new Temple had involved Bro Schutte in more work than he had contracted for, and it was agreed to pay him for this.'

The trio of Thibault, Schutte and Anreith had obviously reaped huge benefits from their collaboration on the lodge building and in the same year worked on Rust-en-Vreugde, which is perhaps one of the finest Cape Dutch townhouses, reminiscent of Koopmans de Wet House and not too far off Gabriel's Petit Trianon. Shortly afterwards, Schutte built a residence for himself quite close to the Castle, which he called Hanover House. In 1809, he collaborated with them on the conversion of the Old Slave Lodge into the High Court.

In 1813, Schutte was appointed a Government Sworn Surveyor

and in 1820, the Inspector of Town Buildings. Among his other commissions was the Cape Town Public Library. In 1826 he teamed up with J. Skirrow in an architectural practice, which designed the Nieuwe Kerk in Bree Street. In 1835, aged 74, he married for a second time. He and his new wife had a daughter who died at the age of one. Schutte died on 25 October 1844, by which time his habit of under-quoting had left him insolvent. He received a Masonic funeral, the costs of which were borne by Lodge de Goede Hoop.

Chapter 7
Anton Anreith

'Next!' called the sergeant.

The man shuffled up to the table.

'Name?'

'Anton Anreith.'

'Hometown?'

'Freiburg in Baden.'

'Age?'

'Twenty-two.'

'A bit old to want to join the army.'

Anreith shrugged.

'Wait there for the doctor.'

Anreith was in Utrecht to join the army and get as far away from Freiberg as possible. He felt terrible that he did not go to Reigel first to say goodbye to his family. That would be the first place they would look for him. He would write and have the letter posted after he left so that they would not be able to dissuade him to stay and face the music. He would miss Reigel, the lovely little church. That was really the start; there he would gaze for hours at the frescos and sculptures which one day he knew he would also make. Now he was as far away from Reigel, from Freiburg and Dresden. How long had he been on the road? He had lost count of the days. He first headed east toward Poland, which was in a terrible mess, then worked on a boat down the Elbe to Vienna, then the Danube in Austria, finally the Rhine to Rotterdam. He had no fear of the medical. He was strong and broad-chested, with forearms that bulged from ten years of sculpture.

'Aren't you Thomas Anrit?' a little man chirped next to him.

He was so deep in his own thoughts that he had not noticed him, 'I'm Anreith, Anton Anreith.'

'I've delivered stone to Wenzinger's Studio in Freiberg and seen you there. Pieter Heinkler, that's me. You even helped me unload once.'

Anton was angry with himself and most of the world, including this little man. What a fool he had been to do that to the sculpture; it was why he was in the mess he was. He hated his sculpture of the Burgermeister just as much as he hated the man. He could see a glimmer of integrity in the work; it was taking on a presence, even looked a bit like him. Wenzinger showed the man and, worse, his wife, while Anreith was burying his father in Reigel. Mrs Burgermeister thought he was more handsome, his nose was much smaller. Then Wenzinger asked Odrano da Cini to adjust it – what a disaster! – and in a blur of anger he reduced it to gravel with a ten-pound hammer. Wenzinger must have been furious; thank God he was not there to see it. He was sure Wenzinger had the police after him and he wondered if he was clear by now. Could they bring him back from Holland?

'Next! Next! Are you deaf?'

Heinkler nudged him in the ribs. The doctor banged on his chest, listened to his heart, scribbled something on a file and sent him on his way with the tiniest swing of his head towards another door. Another queue, winding behind the stables, was being issued uniforms. Finally, his arms full, he headed for the barracks which had racks and racks of beds, two-high, a tin chest in front of each.

Heinkler beckoned him over. 'I've kept you a bed next to me in the corner.'

'Thanks,' nodded Anreith, who shook out a blanket and slept a broken sleep specially reserved for troubled minds.

Days rolled into one as they endured basic training through the damp countryside. Then one day news spread that they were headed for the Cape. Anreith was proud of his smart and efficient company as they marched with their kit on their back to Vreswijk where they took a boat down to Lek. They were getting somewhere at last. From there they headed for Rotterdam, which was a hive of excitement with people everywhere. They went straight to the harbour where the smallish three-master *Woestduijn* was waiting for them. They were set to sail the following morning and while the rest headed into town for a night of revelry, Anreith sought out St Laurens Cathedral for its fine sculptures before going in search of the works of the old masters, Rembrandt, Hals and van Dijk.

Twelve weeks later they docked in Cape Town harbour and his company was billeted in the Castle. The bars and brothels of the back-streets, like any other port, were major attractions to the majority of the sailors and soldiers. The Castle was a great five-sided space divided in two. The rooms, including barracks, were built into the forty-foot-thick walls between the bastions. In the beginning he did burgher watch duty, like in a sort of police force. Anreith would not volunteer for anything, but was ordered to do carpentry for the new hospital.

'I'm no carpenter; I'm a soldier,' complained Anreith.

'You'll learn soon enough,' was the only reply he got.

In no time his talent shone through and he was made a house

carpenter. In his spare time he would roam Cape Town with his sketch book, drawing the buildings, the shaded streets, the mountain, whatever caught his eye. He found comfort in his church, but it was awkward being a Lutheran. Ryk Tulbach, the previous Governor, had declared the Lutheran church 'unrecognised' and therefore not permitted as a religion. When Anreith arrived, there were meetings in houses of many influential merchants, traders and farmers who supported the church, none more so than Martin Melck, one of the richest men in the Cape, who continuously campaigned for recognition.

It was at one of these house meetings that Margretha Melck, martin's daughter, befriended Anreith. She was no beauty and a bit overweight, but Anreith was comfortable with her. Her father became impatient with Ryk Tulbach's edicts and eventually bought three stands in Strand Street and started to build a warehouse that looked suspiciously like an ugly church. Acting Governor van Plettenberg used to say 'when I pass it I keep my nearest eye closed.' Obviously he was caught between a rock and a hard place, so he did what any good governor would do and persuaded the Heeren XVII to rescind the ruling, which they did in 1780. Martin Melck was happy to donate the building to the congregation for a church and Margretha, who had seen Anreith's drawings, persuaded her father and the congregation to engage him to put a new facade on the building. They agreed and the results were pleasing. When the new organ was bought, Margretha wanted Anreith to decorate it. She found her moment on one of their picnics.

'My dear, I'm not a sculptor.'

'Fiddlesticks,' she snapped. Had Heinkler been jawing off?

'I can't do it.'

'For me you'll do it,' she cooed, as some of her father's sheep wandered a little closer to nibble at the fresh grass under the tree.

He really did like her, not love, as he heard others describe it, but he was comfortable with her. She did not usually push as she was now doing.

'Seriously, I'm a carpenter.'

'Nonsense, look at your church facade. It's beautiful,' she cajoled. 'Think about the money; we could do something with that.'

How could he deny her? The Company was happy for him to take on private jobs – though he was still officially a soldier who 'did carpentry' – provided that he did not neglect his work.

'Alright, I'll try,' he muttered, lost in thought.

She smiled to herself.

Things were going well for Anreith. He had been promoted to auxiliary lieutenant of the artillery and then lieutenant in the burgher cavalry. He had been paid for the church, and now the organ loft. Themes haunted his sleep: muses, musicians from the Bible, choirs of angels, the Song of Solomon, but he kept coming back to King David. It was not his best work, he knew that. He was rusty, very rusty. He stuck with King David playing a harp, flanked between two cherubs; he could make them do anything and get away with it. The church loved it, Cape Town loved it; it was the first really world-class sculpture in the Cape. The church was so delighted they commissioned him to do the pulpit. Let my friend George Kendall describe it for you:

> The pulpit is supported by two larger-than-life Herculean figures and two mastiffs. The lectern in front of the pulpit is shaped in the form of a lyre on top of which is the Lutheran swan, wings outstretched to support the volume of the sacred law. Overhead is an intricately worked canopy

surmounted by another Lutheran swan as though on a nest. A lion sits underneath the pulpit – not an integral part of the support but probably to fill the void between the two Herculean figures. A typical Anreithian cherub supports the pastor's lectern, in the pulpit itself, with two further cherub heads to complete the symmetry.

Anreith's sketch of the pulpit details and estimate still survives, one of the only remaining works from his own hand. It took him two years and he was paid 500 rixdollars. Like the hubris of a Greek tragedy he was at the top of his fortunes when the most bitter blow befell him. Margretha left for Holland.

'Why?'

'My father wants me to go to finishing school,' she sobbed.

'I thought we had a future, perhaps marriage,' he stumbled.

'My father doesn't think we're right together.'

'What?'

'He of all people!' she blurted. 'He came here himself as a soldier and married my mother from one of the richest families, and now he objects to you.'

'Why now? Why let us go on for so long?'

'While you had nothing you were no threat.'

'Leave him and live with me.'

'I can't, it would kill mommy,' she said, running off.

It was the last time he saw her.

Shortly afterwards, the French navy arrived in Cape Town 'to offer the Governor their protection', but actually to take over. They did little more than confuse everyone, particularly his boss, the Scottish Colonel Robert Gordon who was in charge of the defences. They did add a little flamboyance to the fashions, then the war in Europe came to an end and they left. Or most of them left and the Government of the Cape once again reverted to the VOC. Compared to losing Margretha, these events had hardly any effect on his life. His friend Heinkler had left for Ceylon and he was utterly alone. He carried on stoically and professionally, doing his job and not allowing anyone to affect him until there was a knock on his door.

He reluctantly tore himself away from his book and went to open it. Hanging onto the opening leaf and deliberately blocking the interior, he stared out at an elegant man of his own age. It was one of the Frenchmen who came in with de Meuron's regiment just recently. He had never spoken to him before; there had been no need, and he wanted to be left alone. Someone said he was an architect, but had come as a soldier with the rank of military engineer. They had him surveying the Company's buildings.

'Can I come in?' he asked in Dutch heavily overlaid with French.

'What for?' also in Dutch, but with German intonations.

'I want to talk to you,' said the Frenchman, standing his ground.

He was smaller than Anreith, almost frail next to his heavy chest and bulging arms, but he was going nowhere. Anreith started to move, scarcely left a gap, and the Frenchman was inside. He took in the room at a glance and was drawn like a magnet to the drawings that were stuck all over the walls.

'Mmmn, *mais oui*,' he exclaimed, taking a candle.

It was a humble space, a man's space; he could have lived happily in the home he and Margretha had planned, but now there seemed no purpose. He had simply taken this deserted area in the north wall of the Castle and had built himself a space. He had asked no permission and not even Colonel Gordon had challenged his arrogance. He certainly did not need to make excuses to this little Frenchman.

'Wine?' grumped Anreith, starting to pour before he had an answer.

'Yes, yes,' said the Frenchman, his eyes glued to the drawings.

Anreith took his own glass, picked up a book and flopped into his chair.

The Frenchman took no notice of the rudeness and sat on the bed. 'My name is Louis Michel Thibault. Your drawings are magnificent.'

'Look, you didn't come here to talk about my drawings. What do you want?'

'I know you're running away from your past.'

That got Anreith's attention. Was he talking about Margretha or Wenzinger?

'It's none of your business.'

'That may be, but it's mad that you and I do not talk to one another. In a way I'm also running away. We're the only two artists in this colony and I have a proposition for you.'

'What are you talking about? I'm no artist.'

'Rubbish,' snapped Thibault. He walked over to some drawings of the pulpit and stabbed his finger like a sword. 'What's this? It's a magnificent drawing. And the final product is one of the finest works of art I've seen in this country.'

'What do you know?' whispered Anreith hoarsely.

'What do I know? I know the best art the world has to offer, and I'm telling you this is some of the finest! So stop sulking and live again.'

Anreith simply nodded, now allowing Thibault to continue.

'Colver, the pastor of the Lutheran Church wants me to design the parsonage. I want you with me.'

'I won't work for Melck. Not now, not ever. Two-faced bastard.'

'You won't need to. He donated the ground to the church and will have nothing to do with it; he's not even on the council anymore. Now it's over to the pastor, the congregation, me and you.'

Lutheran Church

It was Thibault's first commission. At the time Anreith had no idea how he got it. Colver told him much later that the congregation wanted him, but they were apprehensive about approaching him and were pleased when Thibault insisted on bringing him on board. The building turned out very pleasing and it fitted well with the church and helped round off a comfortable complex. After this, Thibault and Anreith became a team that was to last until Thibault's death, by which time they had made some of the loveliest buildings the country has seen. Their success on the Lutheran church channelled a flood of work their way. The first was the Kat

Balcony for the VOC. It was a small architectural job, but one in which Anreith's work shone, the richly carved timberwork setting a benchmark that has never been equalled. The coat of arms is charming, even humorous in its free expression, with cherubs gambolling with armour, or caught in swags and wreaths whilst supporting a shield.

Anreith commandeered more of the space in the wall between the Leerdam and Orange bastions, next to his old apartment, for a workshop for himself, Thibault, Schutte and van Graaf, the head carpenter. Thibault was already a Freemason. He made friendships with some of the members of the defunct Lodge de Goede Hoop, especially Duminy. De Lille, their immediate military superior, was a Mason and finally they decided to start the lodge again. Thibault nagged Anreith to join and he liked the Masons – Zorn the Councillor, de Smit the property owner, Acker, Adriaanessen, Blankenberg were frequent visitors to the workshop. They liked to see his work, but they really came to visit Thibault.

'What the hell, I'll join,' he finally agreed.

Anreith enjoyed the initiation. Over time Freemasonry started to appeal to him, its intent creeping into his understanding. He was intrigued by the metaphors of the rituals, a performance, really, of lessons in moral conduct. Even more than this he enjoyed being with the members at their dinners and socials. There was camaraderie in the army, but here were men who cared about him and worked toward the betterment of themselves and society. And he found a friend in the young fiscal, Truter, who had also just joined.

At the time there were persistent whispers of war in Europe. Literally out of the blue the British navy arrived on the shores of False Bay and Commissioner Sluysken called them out. Anreith's burgher cavalry dashed off to Muizenberg, only to find that it was all over by the time they got there. Most of the burghers had no stomach for it, because they still bore allegiance to the House of Orange, who were friends of the British. Admiral Elphinstone and General Craig had it all wrapped up within days. Everyone's life was confused, they did not know if they still had a job and, if so, who they worked for. Anreith withdrew into himself and went about his business as if nothing had happened. Thibault was under terrible stress as Inspector of Government Buildings as it was his responsibility to account for all the buildings and fortifications to Captain Bridges. He felt for his buildings as if any flaws were his own fault. They even 'borrowed' his maps to complete their reports.

Silence

Their big break came during this period when Truter bought the Garden Domberg to build a new temple for the lodge. He remembered the first time he presented the drawings of his sculptures. They were in Truter's beautiful dining room; Thibault laid out the plans and although he had seen them develop over the last week they suddenly began to live in his imagination. Suddenly they were both looking at him. He always fumbled when he had to sell himself, so Thibault came to his rescue and unfolded his ink stained drawings.

Truter murmured, 'We're getting there.'

'No, you must see "Silence", feel his presence. Feel his pain as he sees his best friend lost in the wilderness and he does not know how to reach out and help him. Feel his strength carrying the load of his brother. Feel his restraint when he himself has been hurt and has every right of rebuke, but restrains himself.'

Anreith hoped that Thibault caught the hidden message as it related to them.

'And this one?' asked Truter, trying to dilute the passion that came flowing into the room.

Grief

'"Grief",' replied Anreith as if that was enough, but they waited. 'It tells of loss and sadness, it is a mother and child, an old theme; every artist that has ever lived has done the Christ child on his mother's lap looking out on us, on the world. I wanted something different. They are concerned for one another, consoling one another as both will suffer and they know it. But we also need consoling and our consolation lies in their care for one another.'

Anreith sat back exhausted from the explanation and frustrated because the words did not convey enough.

'Yes, let's do it,' said Truter. 'These are lovely. I'd like to have drawings of all seven by St John's Day.'

The building went well, even though Thibault often shouted and threw his arms in the air. Schutte shrugged, changing the subject to costings and time. Thibault was going through a hard time: Lady Anne Barnard had returned to England and George Yonge had confiscated his maps. He was trying to get them back, which meant he sat at Government House while there was work to be done. Moreover, Yonge's equally arrogant secretary, Blake, was trying to hijack Freemasonry away from Lodge de Goede Hoop. Then came news that Commissary Abraham de Mist was coming to take back the Cape for the Batavian Republic amid rumours that he was going to shake up Freemasonry. All this caused Thibault to stomp around like a bear with a sore head, leaving a terrible atmosphere in the workshop. Then the roles were reversed when Anreith was snubbed at the consecration.

'Speak to me, for God's sake!' yelled Thibault, sweeping Anreith's drawings off the work bench with his three-cornered hat.

Anreith took a large swig of Hendrik Cloete's brandy from a half-empty bottle and continued staring at his clay models, which he had arranged in a row. Then for some reason only he knew, he rearranged the beautiful little female figures of Faith, Hope and Charity and dropped his head on his arm to see them better. Thibault took a slug of the brandy, pulled up a chair and lowered himself to Anreith's level to stare at the little figures. They were beautiful.

'I don't care about medals, *mon ami*. Here, have mine,' said Thibault, grabbing at his, which was still hanging around his neck.

'The Cape has never seen such work.'

'And will never see it again,' added Thibault. 'So pull yourself together. De Mist was confused and clearly angry; everyone could see he was waiting for another medal to present to you.'

'Oh! I don't think de Mist had anything to do with it.'

'Look, the committee were annoyed with you for not finishing all the pieces, but there was no spite.'

'They know there's no stone here and they wouldn't bring me any. How big a deal would it have been to bring me some from France? They brought bricks for Schutte! And I needed to build the sculptures into the niches and couldn't start until you two were nearly finished. Schutte was nearly six months late. Was I supposed to start before the roof was on? Well, was I?'

Thibault could see that the conversation was heading away from him and took another slug of brandy, 'I'll see you get your medal.'

Anreith completed the seven pieces, four of which were destroyed in the disastrous fire of 1892. And he did receive his medal after the fiery first meeting of the lodge in its new home.

'Brethren, without putting too fine a point on the issue,' said the Master, 'you may recall that we took a vote on the matter. You may also recall that I counselled you against not giving Anreith a medal but that you were so frustrated that you voted against giving him one.'

'Look, Brother Truter, we were angry. He had not completed half of the sculptures and did not deserve a medal.'

'I think the sculptures we have are splendid and we want him to complete his contract. I still think we must give him a medal. They are the best sculpture we have seen in the Cape and I believe we should make a fuss as each piece is finished, perhaps invite schools and church groups in to see them. I will explain it to him if you agree.'

'Agreed, agreed!'

The lodge building was a great success and Truter and Anreith renewed their friendship, working together on numerous projects. His teak carving at Rust-en-Vreugde and the pediments at the new Supreme Court were triumphs.

On one of the pediments he has the Royal Standard surmounted by a crown on a shield supported by a unicorn awake and friskily emerging from the waves and a lion just arisen which lends a paw in steadying the Shield of Justice. The other has the Royal Standard on a glory of spreading rays with the unicorn still emerging from the waves, but it is more interested in the lion that has lost interest in the whole thing and is sleeping or sulking or dead – forecasting the end of the British lion in South Africa. It was an incredible tribute to his eminence as a sculptor that no one thought to tear it down at the time.

——◆——

Thibault, Schutte and Anreith shared a dream of building a school for local craftsmen: Thibault often led the charge, Schutte was always encouraging, but Anreith was the man with the skills to make it happen. They knew Truter was interested in education as he was forever trying to get schools established, nagging everyone for donations for the education fund. The three of them decided to try to harness his energy and experience in their goal.

The studio had never been neater. The ubiquitous dust had been swept and Anreith was moving some of his smaller works to one side when Truter arrived. He was followed by the lawyers, Neethling and Buyskes.

'Schutte will be here soon, but I think we should make a start,' announced Thibault. 'We're deeply honoured that you could come to our humble studio to share our dream.'

'Perhaps you'd be kind enough to tell us what you have been dreaming about,' said Truter.

Schutte sneaked in, hoping no one would notice he was late, but someone whispered, 'as usual'.

'Ah! Yes! As I was about to say...' continued Thibault.

'We want to start a school,' blurted Anreith.

Thibault gave him a wounded look. 'As I was about to say, we believe that we must start a school. And we want the lodge to sponsor it.'

'This is a most admirable sentiment,' observed Truter. 'I've always been keen on starting a school in the Cape. You know that I have the highest regard for your talents, but academically...'

'No, we want a technical school,' cut in Anreith. 'I've been teaching a few students for six years. There's real talent here and I have high hopes for them.'

'We need trained craftsmen,' added Schutte.

'Yes, I can see that it would be a good thing, but as the Master of the lodge I don't see it as our problem,' said Neethling. 'Truter, could you talk to the Governor? He's your friend.'

'Yes I could, but I like what I'm hearing.'

'John, it's their responsibility,' persisted Buyskes.

'They won't do it,' said Truter. 'We have the educational fund, which we could use. Where will you find teachers? What will it cost? Where will you house it?'

'Anton is a brilliant teacher,' said Thibault.

'My pupils Hertzog, Auret and Teubes will help,' said Anreith.

'Could it cost 4 000 rixdollars a year?' asked Truter.

'Has any lodge anywhere in the world ever owned a school?' probed Neethling.

'As operative lodges, we have always taught our own,' said Truter.

'There are many coloured men with talent who are hungry to learn,' said Schutte.

'We'll call it the Masonic Institution,' announced Thibault.

'Let's give it a try,' said Truter. 'I'm not a rich man, but I'll personally donate 4 211 rixdollars over three years. If it doesn't work by then we'll stop it.'

Within a month a meeting was called. The Master, Johannes Henoch Neethling, gavelled the desk in front of him, 'Brethren, can we come to order? We've been contemplating the constitution of a Masonic Education Fund, which will have two goals: To assist young people associated with Freemasonry, our children, and other deserving causes; and to set up a Trade School for craftsmen. We are ready to start it. Brother Truter has spoken to the other lodges; Brother de Wet has dealt with Government; and a few of us have canvassed other parties. We propose to go public tomorrow if you agree. Brother Zorn, will you read the present pledges?'

'These are the subscribers who have agreed and the amounts

they have promised,' said Zorn. 'They will be published in the *Cape Town Gazette* on 23 October:

The High Chapter (Kadosh)	300 rixdollars
The Chapter of the East (and annually 25 rd	200 "
The Scottish Lodge (St Andre d'Afrique annually 100 rd)	300 "
The Lodge of Good Hope (and annually100 rd)	200 "
The British Lodge of Freemasons	350 "
Ancient Masonic Lodge no 354	160 "
Freemasons' Lodge de Goede Hoop	400 "
Freemasons' Lodge de Goede Trouw	650 "
John Andries Truter (over three years)	4 211 "
His Excellency Sir J. F. Craddock	300 "
Rt Hon Lady Theodosia Craddock	200 "

And many individual donations amounting to a total of 4 210 rixdollars and annual donations of 1 835.'

There was a silence in the room, which was shattered by applause.

'Brethren, thank you for that approbation,' said Neethling. 'I knew you would agree and now we want to propose our first candidate for assistance.'

So the Masonic Institution was born. It was the first technical college and the first school of fine art in the country, with Anreith as its first principal. He served in this capacity until his death in 1822. He had very advanced ideas for his times, believing in a relaxed atmosphere. On one occasion he stated that 'compulsion and discipline can only harm real talent.' He wanted students to come and go as they pleased, or, for those who had jobs and could only study part time, whenever best suited them. He requested the lodge to let them have free entry into the Freemasons' temple so that they could enjoy the sight of the statues and architecture there: 'They will learn more in half an hour in there than they would from a month's teaching.'

Anreith's old friend, Thibault, was always there to support him and was often called in to teach. A year after Thibault died, Anreith arranged an exhibition of students' work; the first art exhibition in South Africa. Anreith died seven years after Thibault, at the age of 68. The *Cape Town Gazette* reported the funeral as follows:

> He was a late officer in the auxiliary Artillery, and latterly head instructor of the Freemasons' Educational Institution. His great abilities in Mathematics, Architecture, Sculpture, Drawing etc were well known; and the loss of so valuable a member of society will be deeply regretted by a large circle of friends. The funeral took place from the Goede Hoop Lodge: The coffin was conveyed from the Temple to the Hearse by six of his pupils and six members of the lodge were pall bearers. The procession was numerously and respectably attended.

Anreith was buried in the old Military Cemetery, which has long since been deconsecrated and built over. Of him we have virtually nothing as he was a very self-effacing man – very few contemporary references, no portrait or description, and very little by his own hand. Yet, in the silence of the Temple of the Lodge de Goede Hoop, some of his most splendid works remain 208 years later. May they continue to do so for many centuries to come as they are the splendid works of South Africa's first Masonic sculptor for all South Africans. Call there any time, knock on the door and ask the tyler (caretaker) to show you around, which he will gladly do for a small donation to charity.

Author's Note: My friend, George Kendall, delivered a paper in Lyceum Lodge of Research on Wednesday 17 February 1982, entitled Anton Anreith: South Africa's First Masonic Sculptor, which is the foundation of this story and a memorial to him. It is he who sparked my interest in these men and this period.

Wood carving to the Balcony
Door First Floor
Rust-en-Vreugd

Part 3

The Spread

Chapter 8
Christoffel Josephus Brand

There was a knock at the door. Johannes looked at his father, Oupa Christoffel Brand, but he was busy with his bobotie and pretended not to notice. Johannes's wife shrugged her shoulders while her son Christoffel flashed a look at his brother Philipus. Their little sisters did not bother with the intrigue and jumped off their chairs and raced for the door. It was a rare occurrence that anyone called at dinner time.

'Uncle John, Uncle John,' the girls squealed in delight.

Truter walked into the room with the two girls around his neck and Johannes Neethling following with a bemused look on his face. Everyone he knew was intimidated by Truter's piercing eyes and distant reserve; you shook his hand never dreaming of giving him a hug, but these girls had no such hesitation.

'Sorry, I didn't realise you'd be dinning,' apologised Neethling. 'Oom Christoffel suggested we come about now.'

Everyone stared at Oupa Christoffel, who feigned surprise, 'Hello John, Johannes. I'm sorry, but it's the only time we're all here.'

'Come sit, you two. There's plenty of bobotie,' said Wilhelmina. Pointing a wooden spoon at her father-in-law, she said, 'I'll deal with you later.'

No, no,' they sang in unison.

'Sit!'

The children shifted up while the young Christoffel went to find glasses. When he returned, his mother sent him back for fancier ones, into which his father poured wine for the visitors while Wilhelmina dished up bobotie garnished with peach chutney, grated coconut and banana.

'We bring good news,' said Truter, looking first at Wilhelmina then young Christoffel. 'The education fund will sponsor your education in Leyden.'

'I don't understand,' said Wilhelmina.

'I made application on Christoffel's behalf,' confessed Oupa Christoffel with tears of joy brimming in his eyes. 'The lodge has a fund to help promising young people and they've agreed to help us with Christoffel's further studies.'

'You interfering old man. Who says he wants to go to Leyden?'

'I went to Leyden,' interjected Truter. 'It's a very good university.'

'I was aware of Oupa's application,' said Johannes. 'It will cost 2 475 rixdollars. We have nearly 1 000 rixdollars saved and the lodge will finance the balance.'

⬥

Young Christoffel arrived in Holland early in 1815. He was a bright, nuggety young man with a sharp sense of humour and a shock of blond hair. He adapted easily into the big city life.

Dear Pa,
Leyden is everything Uncle John said it was and more.

I stopped in Amsterdam for a day and walked my feet off. That opened my eyes and I must go back there. Uncle John's friend arranged a carriage to Leyden, where I am happily ensconced in my digs. Being a junior anywhere is, I suppose, the same. Some here would like to have the better of me, but I will not allow it though I now think I might allow a few liberties so that I do not seem too off-ish.

I let it be known that my family are the pillars of the lodge and that I have a letter of introduction from Uncle John. I told them it was from the Grand Master National and I have already had an approach from Lodge la Vertu here in Leyden. I have met a few of them and it looks as if I'll be joining them.

Your son

◆

Dear Christoffel

Thank you for your note and I am happy to tell you we are all well.

I am pleased you are joining a lodge as it has always been a source of great joy to me and Oupa. I have been made the Government Representative in Stellenbosch, and we have moved to the official residence there, so I don't get to lodge much. I don't mind working for the British as I keep telling myself that they are here with the blessing of Prince William of Orange. Oupa Christoffel is living in our house in Cape Town with Philipus and the girls so that their schooling will not be affected.

You may recall that three years ago we applied for a warrant for an English lodge. We had almost forgotten about the petition when it arrived in the name of 'The Hope Lodge No 727'. It is an English Lodge, but owned by de Goede Hoop. It follows our bylaws; all revenues after expenses are remitted to de Goede Hoop; and a member can claim membership of one or both lodges. It was constituted by Uncle John and there was a splendid dinner and table lodge proceeded by the usual procession in the lodge grounds, in which all lodges in Cape Town took part.

They now want to extend this arrangement to include a lodge under the banner of the Grand Orient of France. It all started when brethren of de Goede Hoop wanted to open and operate a Rose Croix Chapter and applied to the Grand Orient of France for a warrant. This was agreed provided that a craft lodge was opened under the same constitution and Lodge l'Esperance was formed on the same basis as the Hope Lodge. Many of the members belong to all three lodges. To put it another way, we have in effect a lodge which could work under three Grand Lodge constitutions.

You will be pleased to know that Uncle John has received a knighthood; the first *Kaapenaar* to ever have been so honoured. I am pleased your studies are coming together, keep it up.

Your loving father

At the age of 18, Christoffel joined Lodge la Vertu in Leyden. This was unusual as normally a man would have to be 21 years old to join a lodge except if he was the son of a Mason (called a lewis) and then he would usually only be accepted into the father's lodge. The only way this could otherwise take place would be by compelling letters of introduction. There he also obtained two doctorates for his theses *The Relationship of the Colonies to the Mother Country* and *Questions in Socratis Sententium de Deo*. After completing his studies he returned to the Cape in 1821 to set up a law practice. He was to find it subtly changed since he had left.

The British had initially left everything as it was. The new colonisers could not afford to alienate the burghers, especially the more influential ones, as this would have pushed up the cost of occupation. But they slowly began to reform labour policies and shift to anglicisation. Truter was foremost amongst the leading officials in trying to get the populace to accept change, especially with regard to slavery. There had also been a steady shift eastwards and the eastern frontier had come up against the Xhosa nation, raising tensions there. Troubles intensified, culminating in the attack on Grahamstown by the mystic Makana and 10 000 followers on 22 April 1819. Governor Lord Charles Somerset had called for Britain to send emigrants to bolster the defences of the colony and these appeals now became more urgent. Britain, in the grip of depression since the end of the Napoleonic wars in 1815, seized the opportunity to rid itself of some of its excess population. Farms and transport were offered for nearly 4 000 men, women and children through advertisements that focused more on Somerset's extravagant claims that the eastern Cape resembled 'a succession of parks in which, upon the most verdant carpet, nature has planted in endless variety' rather than warning of the risks involved.

Leyden had confirmed Brand's Dutchness, but on his return he was to find English the official legislative language. However mild the changes, these were rules formulated in England and which had to be followed. He was offended by this shift and became vehemently opposed to this willy-nilly erasing of his language and culture. He also started attending Lodge de Goede Hoop by virtue of his membership of Lodge la Vertu. And he met Cartharina Fredrica Kuchler.

'Do you, Cartharina Fredrica Kuchler, take Christoffel Josephus Brand as your lawfully wedded husband?'

'I do.'

'Do you...'

The Moederkerk in Stellenbosch was hot in December 1822. You could hear the clop of hoofs on the cobbles outside above the incessant buzz of cicadas. After the service the couple were in a blur of their own: Cartharina was all he ever wanted and an exciting future lay before them. Table three at the reception could easily have been mistaken for the Board of General Purposes of Lodge de Goede Hoop.

'They make a wonderful couple,' observed Truter.

'I think he's a young man we should cultivate, and she'll help him,' added Carl van Breda.

Truter turned to Neethling. 'What are your plans, Johannes? You've been Master for ten years. I think you've been the best we've ever had, but you must be thinking of a successor.'

'John, are you trying to get rid of me?'

'You know me better than that, Johannes. I have plans for you. I want you in the Provincial Grand Lodge I plan to form, and you've hinted you'd like to step aside.'

'I do know you better than that, but I smell a plot growing in your head. Out with it.'

'I see that young man going far in Freemasonry, so we must get him started on the ladder of promotion.'

'I may have a solution,' suggested Frouenfelder. 'I've been secretary for a long time and would like to retire. Let's make him secretary.'

'Good idea,' said van Breda. 'We can then give him a few years then make him Master.'

'Johannes, you should actively mentor him over the next few years,' said Truter. 'I think we must also draw his father back into the lodge. Give him a job.'

In June 1823, Brand was made secretary of the lodge when Brother Frouenfelder retired. Brand's first child, Johannes Hendricus, was born on 11 January 1824: little could they have imagined then that he would be a future president of the Orange Free State and one of the great sons of South Africa. It is known the boy was stubborn and did not easily bend to authority. His early education was from tutors and society schools and when he was fifteen, he was sent to the South African College (SACS). There he met a coloured boy, David Arnot, who would later feature in his life. Like his father, he would become an enthusiastic Freemason and be sent to study in Leyden through the education fund. He would go on to London to complete his education at the Inner Temple and be admitted to the bar before being drawn home by love.

Christoffel Brand was becoming increasingly disillusioned with British rule by decree. There was little representation and no free press. Ironically, the first concerted opposition came from the English press. Editors Thomas Pringle, John Fairbairn, Abraham Faure and George Greig took up the cudgels against English authority between 1824 and 1826. Brand joined them in securing the rights to a license to publish, engage in political discussion and report on the actions of Government.

'But Uncle John, there must be something we can do about it,' said Christoffel.

'We are doing something about it,' responded Truter.

'What?'

'Well, we all have different roles to play. I am old and, I hope, wise, and must use what talents I've got to do what I think is best. You, on the other hand, are young and bright and must use your energy appropriately. I've heard that you are trying to form a cultural society – Zuid-Afrikaansche Athenaeum. I think that's admirable.'

'It's hardly going to frighten the British.'

'I also hear you've taken an interest in politics. Provided you handle it intelligently, that too is admirable. I have always believed in a quiet revolution, appeal to people's minds. Those who blow things up usually blow themselves up. Your newspaper friends have made great strides. I think you should write more; establish your own newspaper in Dutch.'

The *Zuid-Afrikaan* newspaper was established in 1830 with Christoffel as its editor and Truter as his mentor. Over the next quarter century the British bent before the storm brought on by the editors and introduced many reforms. Among these were changes to the legal system. Up to now British officials had administered justice; this responsibility was passed to magistrates and a system of jury trials. A decision-making Executive Council was followed by representative government, the distribution of Crown land at the Governor's discretion was revised, and the administration of justice was remodelled. The latter was the last major judicial assignment Truter worked on. He waited to see the new system introduced and then at the age of 65 retired on a pension of £600 a year.

In June 1832 Brand declined re-election as secretary of Lodge de Goede Hoop. The bylaws stipulated a limit of six years in office and he had already served that long. The Master, van Breda, held that a unanimous vote would override this, but Brand disagreed, and Brother Stroedel was elected. Stroedel, though, died sixteen months later and Brand again filled the secretary's seat. He set an example of carefully recording, documenting and archiving the records, which are today among the oldest in the state archives. In 1836 he was appointed orator and gave a notable address dwelling on the past history of Freemasonry in South Africa and congratulating the brethren who were celebrating anniversaries. And on 24 June 1837 he was made Master of the lodge, thus continuing a long family association.

Cape Freemasonry was still governed directly by Holland. No one had a real problem with this other than it made day-to-day administration cumbersome. New lodges were being formed and there was the potential to form many more, but the system had to be made manageable. Truter proposed the establishment of a Provincial Grand Lodge, a sort of branch office, that would iron out these issues. On 18 August 1838 this became a reality with Truter as Provincial Grand Master and the Hon Michiel van Breda as Deputy Provincial Grand Master. All the posts on this body, except for that of B. de Roos who became Provincial Grand Junior

Warden, were held by members of Lodge de Goede Hoop.

The English lodges decided to do likewise and combined to form the Provincial Grand Lodge of the Grand Lodge of England. Then came a curious move. The Brethren of the Hope Lodge then petitioned the Grand Lodge of England to appoint John Truter as Provincial Grand Master for the Grand Lodge of England. The Grand Lodge of England agreed. All the English lodges combined to form the Provincial Grand Lodge at the temple at eleven o'clock. Thereafter they marched behind the band of the 72nd Regiment to the Dutch Reformed Church where the divine service was read by the Reverend Fearan Fellows (HM Astronomer at the Cape). Truter was installed and held that office for the next ten years. He was the equivalent of District Grand Master of two grand lodges at the same time and it has been suggested that this was the first attempt to form a united Grand Lodge in South Africa, but, like so many attempts that followed, it failed.

———•———

While Christoffel was making progress in Masonry, his professional and political activities were not left behind. Ellison Kahn tells the following delicious story:

> The subject matter of the suit is immaterial, but the counsel was – or so the story goes – the late Christoffel Brand, a small man. His client, the plaintiff, who understood no English and was a veritable Anak (giant), sat behind him. When it came to the argument Brand got up and after he had said a few words the court intimated that it did not wish to hear him, so he sat down again. This meant, as

everyone in court but the client knew, that he would in all probability win his case.

Counsel on the other side made a gallant fight: there were many points put by the court which were strenuously combated. The argument took a long time and was continued without any loss of spirit.

Meanwhile Brand's client was becoming more restless and had audibly expressed the most palpable dissatisfaction when his counsel had sat down with hardly a word. What the other side had been saying was incomprehensible to him, but this he did not understand. That counsel had been talking for more than an hour and His Lordship was not interrupting him any longer was a sign he naturally misinterpreted.

At last he could endure it no longer. He rose to his great height, bent over and seizing Brand by his trousers' seat, lifted him high up as he shouted, '*Weer jou, mij kleintje, weer jou, ons verloor die zaak.*' ('Defend yourself, my little man, defend yourself, we are losing the case.')

Brand found himself at odds with the English press. They championed representative government and the abolition of slavery, but Brand prevaricated on endorsing abolition. This led Fairbairn to believe that abolition would not happen if preceded by representative government and that it should happen by decree. The issue of slavery was at the time a very emotive issue for the burghers and came to be the focus of dissatisfaction with British rule. It culminated in one of the most momentous events in South African history.

> History has seldom witnessed a stranger and more moving spectacle than that of well-to-do farmers, some in their first flush of youth and others already bending under the weight of years, forsaking their farms and homesteads, packing their families with all their household goods into the unwieldy ox-wagon, driving their flocks and herds before them, and trekking into the distant unknown interior.

So wrote Dutch Reformed minister Andrew Murray. The myth-makers of Afrikaner nationalism morphed the Great Trek into a biblical exodus – of a chosen people leaving in search of Canaan. It was nothing of the sort. Rather, it was primarily a rebellious search for more land by a group of fractious, independently minded and predominantly eastern Cape burghers fed up with encroaching British authority. Notwithstanding, the migration of a significant number of well-armed people with specific ideas about racial superiority into an interior already in turmoil was to have a massive impact on southern African history.

'We quit this colony under the full assurance that the English Government has nothing more to require of us, and will allow us to govern ourselves without interference in future,' declared one leader, Piet Retief, as he left Grahamstown.

It was wishful thinking as, in late 1835, hundreds of *kakebeen* (jawbone) ox-wagons – with the bearded, grizzled patriarch dressed in button-down jacket, corduroy *klapbroeke* and *veldskoene* perched on the *wa-kist* and women in bonnets and flowing black cloaks behind – began creaking away from towns and dorps in the Cape on an epic journey beyond the border. Here they fanned out, most choosing to continue either into the central interior or north-east over the Drakensberg into present day KwaZulu-Natal with its safe harbour that promised access to a sympathetic outside world. The most significant of the groups that chose the coast were headed by Gerrit Maritz and Piet Retief, who arrived in late 1837, and those under Piet Uys and Andries Pretorius that followed shortly afterwards.

Trouble started straight away. Firstly, there was dissension among the trekkers when Retief's followers elected him chief leader and supreme military commander. And secondly, Zulu king Dingaan took fright at the arrival of large numbers of settlers, which led to the massacre of Retief and the ambushing of Uys before the Zulus were defeated at Blood River on 16 December 1838. After this the Trekkers declared the short-lived Republic of Natalia with Pretorius as president and Pietermaritzburg in the Umzunduze Valley as capital.

Natalia, later shortened to Natal, was taken by the British in 1842 and annexed as a dependency of the Cape Colony in 1845, so most of the Boers again trekked. Susanna Smit, a sister of Gerrit Maritz, declared: 'We will never submit to British authority. We would rather walk out by the Drakensberg barefooted, to die in freedom, as death is dearer than the loss of liberty.' Trekkers from Natal moved to the interior to join the Boers who had established a number of republics, primarily the Transvaal and Orange Free State.

While there are those who may think Brand and the burghers who remained in the Cape were intransigent conservatives, he became a leading figure in the popular party that pushed for a more inclusive, representative government. Most of those advocating a more limited franchise came from the English community on the eastern frontier. It is interesting to note that he supported the franchise for all who met the requirements, regardless of race, which was extremely enlightened for the time. In 1840 he was elected to the first Cape Town Executive Committee and later to the first colonial legislature, where he became speaker.

——•——

In June 1834 Michiel van Breda was in the chair of Lodge de Goede Hoop when all the Masons in the Cape gathered for a special ceremony to celebrate Truter's thirty years as Deputy Grand Master. The brethren presented a portrait of him in oils to the lodge, which unfortunately was one of the treasures lost in the fire. Ten years later Truter celebrated his fiftieth year as a Mason; the first South African to do so.

In 1840 Brand vacated the chair and was succeeded by Christiaan Laurens Herman. Brand was quite happy to go back to his old job as assistant orator. In 1842 it was decided to open membership of the Society, the lodge's private club, to non-Masons. It was with great joy to Christoffel that in 1842 his nineteen-year-old son, Johannes Hendricus, while still a student, was initiated as a lewis into Lodge de Goede Hoop. Living in the most Masonic home in the Cape, he was left with few options and became enthusiastically involved and showed an early talent for debate. Little wonder that three years after his initiation he became orator of the lodge, a post he held for thirteen years in total, split by his studies. The Freemasons' Yearbook of 1842 states, 'On 13 January 1842 at the first yearly Masonic Lodge of Sorrows, the student J. H. Brand gave an able address.' In the same year the lodge's education fund provided him with funds to 'prosecute his studies in Leyden'. In March 1843 he started at Leyden University, graduating as a doctor of civil laws. During his time there he made many lifelong friends, in particular Professor Johan Rudolf Thorbecke, who was to become Prime Minister of Holland, and John Louden, who went on to become Governor General of the Dutch East Indies.

———•———

My Dear Johannes,

I am pleased your studies are progressing so well. No small part I am sure is being in Leyden. It is such a thrill for me to hear that you enjoy the same resonance I felt walking in the steps of Rembrandt and William of Orange, and to be able to do so with the friends you describe is wonderful.

I have been persuaded to take the chair again. Uncle John has bullied me into it. I am sorry you will not be here for my installation.

He also tells me that he will be resigning as Deputy Grand Master National and thinks I should take over from him. Look, it is an enormous honour, but also a massive challenge as I am only Master of my lodge. Michiel van Breda is next in line, but has turned down the offer. I think I should take it. What do you think?

Your mother misses you.

Your father, Christoffel J. Brand

In 24 June 1844 Christoffel Brand was made Deputy Grand Master National. Truter did resign and the Dutch lodges were called upon to each nominate three candidates for the next Deputy Grand Master National. Van Breda was asked, but declined. Two lodges put forward Brand's name, but his appointment was delayed for many months. In 1847 Lodge de Goede Hoop celebrated its 75th anniversary, which was again presided over by Brand. Naturally there followed a splendid banquet. In September there was a Lodge of Sorrows, a Masonic memorial service, for van Breda and W. F. Hertzog, Deputy Master of the lodge.

In October, the Dutch warship *Zwaluw* arrived with documents appointing Brand as Deputy Grand Master National for South Africa over both the symbolic and higher degrees. The lodge was so delighted that it initiated the commander as well as the first and second lieutenants of the ship and took them through their first and second degrees for free, which was apparently done on a few occasions. Brand felt he should not be Deputy Grand Master at the same time as he was Master of the lodge and stood down in favour of Brother Overbeek. At a festival in December 1847, Brand was installed in his new position of symbolic Masonry by Overbeek. Baron Carl von Ludwig was due to install him over the higher degrees, but he died on the day and the job was done by Brother J. Tromp. As usual they left a few pages in the minute book to 'write up' the installation but never did. Many years later Brand tried to fill in these gaps from memory. It was at the time of his installation that it was found that many pieces of the lodge's silver collection deposited at the bank had gone missing.

On his return to the Cape, his son Johannes set up practice as an attorney, which by all accounts was a very successful one. It was a curious arrangement; sometimes he worked as junior to his father and on other occasions opposed him in court cases. Like his father, he was drawn to politics. On 11 August 1851 he married Sabilia Zastron. She was a great support to him and as popular as he, with an ability to put people at ease.

Christoffel was undeniably the head of Freemasonry and sought every opportunity to push the order to the fore. When the new Cape parliament was looking for a House of Assembly he offered to rent them Lodge de Goede Hoop's assembly rooms, which were the most handsome in the country. The rental was set at £50 for the first year increasing to £250 in the twentieth year. This brought prestige to the lodge and some income. What other lodge anywhere in the world can claim to have housed their country's parliament for thirty years? It met there for the first time on 30 June 1854.

Christoffel was Speaker of the House and Johannes stood for and was elected as member for Clanwilliam. At this time the younger man was a firebrand. It is worth quoting a journalist of the day who wrote, 'He has plenty of words – indeed there is no end to his words – he is too declamatory, too loud, too vehement but beneath all this, something better lurks.' It was a picture of a young man filled with vigour and fire, eager to do great things, but not knowing how to. He was handsome and charming and this made him less irritating.

There is nothing like Freemasonry to give one a level perspective, and nothing like being Master to smooth over one's rough spots. In 1858 Johannes followed his uncle Philipus as Master of Lodge de Goede Hoop, which was no mean achievement. In those days one had to earn the Mastership, it was not dished out in rotation as it is done today. Neethling held the chair for twenty years, Truter for seven, his father for six and his uncle for five. As Reverend Faure was to say at his funeral, 'It was Freemasonry that made him the man he was,' and being Master was the refining part of that development. He learnt to rule without power, to guide by example, to listen more than talk.

The Brands made a powerful family with two of the sharpest advocates in the land, both members of Parliament, part of a

Masonic dynasty and friends of all the influential people in Cape Town. They met, among others, C. J. Rhodes and Paul Kruger and counted Sir George Grey as a close friend. It was the latter who had a soft spot for the Orange Free State and probably pointed Johannes in that direction. And father and son were busy men. Johannes was at the coal face of Masonry as Master of the lodge and in addition to his parliamentary duties he had a love of teaching, which led him to take the professorship of law at the South African College, which later became the University of Cape Town. During his time there he taught both F. W. Reitz, who followed him as president of the Orange Free State, and N. P. Schriener, who was to become Prime Minister of the Cape. He was present when his father initiated President Pretorius of the Orange Free State as a Mason as well as his secretary, Carl Bredell.

Christoffel Brand left the daily management of Freemasonry to others and they got up to some weird things, but he left them to it. They bought a share in Protecteur Assurance Company; forbade bowls and golf in their society club; contributed to a statue of Laurens Janzoon Coster, the first printer in Holland; made a permanent seat for Christoffel in the lodge; and helped rebury some English soldiers in Grahamstown. A portrait of Brand was donated to the lodge and for the first time the lodge recorded its finances in English currency. While they did this he concentrated his attention on a greater vision: the expansion of Masonry.

The English Provincial Grand Lodge had ceased to function after the death of Clerke Burton, their Provincial Grand Master. By now they had five new lodges with no leadership. After his appointment as Deputy Grand Master National, Brand found his Provincial Grand Lodge was also hardly functioning. The same people were running everything and had the freedom to rule dictatorially.

Brand could see that the country's demographics were being swung by the English settlers and that they naturally drifted into English lodges. Even though he was busy, he knew this problem needed his personal intervention and he set off on the first of three missionary tours of the country. It was not always easy as there was a shortage of Dutch Masons so he roped in the English ones to start new lodges and was happy for Dutch lodges to work in English to encourage candidates from both language groups. He attracted the most senior people into Freemasonry and eventually had twelve lodges to supervise, some as far afield as Potchefstroom in the Transvaal.

Brand's Masonic kingdom was stretching far and wide, further than could be comfortably managed. A move started to form two districts – one in the east, around Port Elizabeth, and the other around the Cape Town base in the west. He invited lodges to comment. The general consensus was that the districts should not be split, because then the Orange Free State and Transvaal would also want a separate district.

On 5 June 1854 Christoffel Brand's old friend and mentor, John Truter, died at the age of 91. His funeral took place five days later and Brand described his funeral in *Die Zuid-Afrikaan*:

> The only wish he had before his departure was that he may be conveyed to the grave by his profession and his colleagues. The desire was nobly responded to. The Bar bore his coffin, and the Bench, together with the

secretary to Government, were the pall bearers. At two o'clock the corpse was brought to town and deposited in the church, where the people, and those who intended to pay the last tribute to departed merit, began to assemble. At the same time several Masonic processions began to assemble, for the purpose of going together to the Lodge de Goede Hoop which was put into deep mourning. The Bar also assembled at the Chamber of the Senior Member, the Hon Advocate Cloete, whence they proceeded, duly robed, towards the church, the legal profession and Masonry vied with each other to honour his remains.

Nine days later Lodge de Goede Hoop held a Lodge of Sorrows in memory of Right Worshipful Brother Sir John Andries Truter. Somerset described him as 'a man of sound judgement and exceptional ability' and William Porter as 'perhaps one of the ablest of the men the Colony has produced.' Like most Masons he saw the church and Freemasonry as institutions working in tandem for the greater good. He devoted much of his attention to the church and was especially interested in furthering missionary work. At a local level he helped establish the congregation in Wynberg and served as its scribe for a number of years and was elected an honorary member of its consistory. At a national level he represented the church as political commissioner and went on to represent the Government at all of the synods. He was a man who saw many of his dreams come true: he was passionately devoted to education and his first experiment was the Masonic Institution, while the establishment of SACS brought him the most joy and he remained on its council for many years to see it properly established.

Seeing Brand's success, the Grand Lodge of England decided to get their Provincial Grand Lodge going again and in 1862 nominated Richard Southey, then Treasurer-General of the Colony, as Provincial Grand Master, and appointed him on 5 March 1863. He faced similar problems to those that confronted Brand. Their dissention centred on a battle between Albany Lodge in Grahamstown and Richard Southey's PGM English constitution. Albany had been agitating for a separate district or warrant from London and refused to submit returns or pay fees. Southey summoned representatives to appear at a meeting on 15 July 1868 'and show cause why they should not be suspended for contumacy.'

Sir Richard Southey

Albany's Master, R. E. Rushby, wrote to London pointing out that Southey's summons was disingenuous. To attend the meeting would take three weeks and cost £50 per person. He added that Freemasonry was languishing in the east as a result of Southey's rule. Southey had already issued a warning, so he suspended them. They then applied for a warrant from the Scottish constitution, which they got. So Southey suspended all communication with the Scottish constitution, which created a ridiculous situation because many Masons belonged to lodges in both constitutions, and the suspension effectively prevented members from visiting their own lodges. This was one of Southey's blunders, but there were many others caused by the fact that his district secretary, W. Rufus Ellis, suppressed letters from lodges (including those from Albany Lodge) that proved them blameless. In 1871 Albany was resuscitated when the Grand Master, the Earl of Zetland, granted a Provincial Grand Lodge to the eastern Cape.

Their lack of success and the confusion with their own leadership was frustrating to many English Masons, some of whom became jealous of Brand and started asking awkward questions about Dutch Freemasonry in South Africa. The kernel of the problem started in 1770 in a convention between England and Holland in which the Grand East of the Netherlands undertook not to constitute any new lodges in any part of the world where lodges were established under the patronage of England.

The English District Grand Master made no comment, but a group a young hotheads questioned the Dutch's right to founding any new lodges. In particular, John Saunders Rowe maintained that, as the Cape was under the patronage of England, Dutch-initiated Masons were irregular. What they seemed to have forgotten was that the Dutch established its Masonic foothold long before the English took over. Brand set out the facts in a masterful statement on 6 March 1867, which everyone called his Masonic Epistle. It was sufficient to convince the Grand Master of England and, more importantly, the Grand Secretary, to let sleeping dogs lie. They agreed that the original convention could not have foreseen the situation that had developed at the Cape.

At the age of 73 Brand set off on yet another missionary journey and established four more lodges while visiting many old ones. In Adelaide he even responded to the unusual request to form an English lodge under the Dutch constitution.

Chapter 9
Marthinus Wessel Pretorius

Marthinus Wessel Pretorius loved to sit on the stoep when the night was still and the stars were bright in the velvet darkness. He could look down on the Crocodile River and the little dam at the end of his farm Kalkheuvel as the moon sketched a path across the water in beaten silver.

He smiled at the crazy things he had done in his life. The Orange Free State episode was probably the maddest of all. He recalled standing in their Volksraad as President of the Transvaal to give his best Boere-unity speech and then demanding possession of their country. They must have thought him insane. There was a deathly silence in the Assembly Hall, so he started to talk more. Even now he was not sure what he said; Goertz said he quoted the promise made by Sir George Cathcart to his father, Andries, the legendary Voortrekker leader and 'Hero of Blood River', as if that had anything to do with it. He remembered going on and on about solidarity and, of course, the English. Then he stopped.

'Mr Speaker, I'm not sure I know what the Honourable President Pretorius has been saying to us,' said H. A. L. Hamelberg, breaking the silence. 'Perhaps he would be kind enough to commit it to writing.'

H.A.L. Hamelberg

There was overwhelming agreement and the Speaker declared the motion carried.

They obviously did not know what to do with him. That was not the first of his attempts: he had gatecrashed their assembly once before with Stander and Venter and demanded they pay him back the £3 000 his father expended on ammunition when he came to their aid in one of their earlier wars with the Basotho. They gave him £1 500 and sent him away. Then he declared his right to protect the Orange Free State burghers and assembled a commando and invaded the place. President Boshoff declared martial law and they ended up facing one another across the Rhenoster River for days on end like two old bulls. He smiled at the memory. At least he got a peace treaty out of them. It was not as easy with his wife Aletta, who said he acted like a bull-at-a-gate. But he loved to stir the waters and let the issues float out. He certainly angered them when he would not help them hoist their new flag. They thought they were honouring him, but he did not approve of them using anything other than the Boer flag.

'Why do they need a new one?' he asked Goertz.

That night he and Goertz sat up half the night drafting his claim, which Hamelberg read the next day in the Volksraad. He made it sound ridiculous and they were again thrown out. Aletta said he was lucky they did not throw them in an asylum. Thank God they did not have one. Then Boshoff resigned and Pretorius's supporters in the Orange Free State saw it as an opportunity and bullied him into standing for election as president in 1859. Cape Governor Sir George Grey warned him that Britain would regard such a union of offices as a violation of the conventions of 1852 and 1854, but Pretorius refused to be dictated to.

Aletta had a field day.

'Have they not got enough for you here with all those little republics?' she demanded.

'Paul Kruger will fix the bits and pieces, now I want to bring the Free Staters into the fold.'

'You've enough trouble running four republics; how will you manage five?'

'Don't you see? Then there'll only be one big republic.'

'What does your Volksraad think of this?'

'They like it. They've even promised me six months' leave of absence if I win.'

Well, he won and he was now the President of the Orange Free State and he was pulling out his hair with his trouble with Basotho monarch Moshweshwe and he was leaving tomorrow for Cape Town to see Sir Philip Wodehouse to sort out the mess.

—•—

There were small sounds from deep in the house which blend-
ed with the friendly chatter of his people in the copse of trees
further down in the valley. Their fire twinkled between the trees;
the women tending their pots and singing their sad songs while the
old men told stories on their haunches and smoked their pipes.
He could just make out some cattle beyond the fence scuffling in
the long grass; he could even smell their clean grassy odour. Somewhere little Chrissie's peacock cried mournfully in the night. Little
Chrissie stole onto the stoep and snuggled onto his lap. He loved
the smell of her hair. Aletta made special soap for it from aloe sap,
essence of roses and rosemary.

'Oupa, what was it like when you were little?' she asked shyly.

'Now where were we last night?'

'You told me about how you learned to read and write and a bit
about the Trek.'

'There were two kinds of Dutch farmers,' he began. 'There were
those who were almost as English as the English on their fancy
farms near Cape Town. They were happy with the Government.
The rest of us Boers were angry with the British and didn't accept
that they had any rights over us, our education, our properties.
And we didn't believe we owed them taxes so we spread further
into the hinterland.'

Pretorius remembered how they had sold their farm in Graaff-
Reinet to English settlers from Albany. They picked them up for
a song, creating even greater resentment. The English had got
their own way and he now wondered if it would not have been
better to fight it out. His family had set off in 1837 and headed for
the Indian Ocean coast where he became president of the Republic of Natalia. But the British had no intention of leaving them be.

The name Natalia, later shortened to Natal, originates with

Vasco da Gama. He sailed past that coast on Christmas Day 1497 and named it Terro do Natalia (Land of the Nativity). In 1823 Lieutenants James King and George Farewell, on a trading expedition to St Lucia Bay, found refuge from bad weather in a bay to the south, which until then was thought blocked by a sand bar. Basing themselves on Salisbury Island at the entrance, they charted what was to become Port Natal. The following year Farewell organised a party under Henry Francis Fynn who obtained a grant of land around the bay from then-Zulu-king Shaka and there established a trading and ivory-hunting post. Among the first to settle here were Alexander Biggar and a very young Richard (Dick) King, who would go on to become 'the saviour of Natal'. The town grew and in June 1835 the residents decided to change its name to D'Urban, in honour of Cape Governor Sir Benjamin D'Urban.

Two years later the Boers arrived, followed soon afterwards by the British at the height of the Trekker struggle with the Zulus. The new Cape Governor, Sir George Napier, had wanted to mark his disapproval of the emigrants' proceedings by throwing as many impediments in their way as he could. 'Accordingly Napier sent a Major Samuel Charters with 100 Highlanders by sea to Port Natal and they landed there without opposition on 4 December 1838,' writes Oliver Ransford in *The Great Trek*.

> Twelve days later, after building a fort [Fort Victoria], and while the Battle of Blood River was still in progress, Charters ran up the Union Jack amid 'tremendous firing both of great guns and small arms'. Afterwards the British officer retired to the mess tent to drink the Queen's health and toast absent friends. There was no question at the time of annexing Natal: Charters was careful to stress

in a proclamation that his occupation of land was limited to two miles from the 'sinuosities of the bay'.

But Napier received little support either from the English settlers or the British Government and towards the end of 1839 instructed the withdrawal from the port. 'The Boers naturally regarded this evacuation as the final abandonment by Great Britain of any claim to Natal,' continues Ransford.

> Durban was reoccupied and the bay resounded again to the noise of gunfire as the horsemen rode in from Pieter-maritzburg, fired off a ragged volley and hoisted the flag of the Natalian republic. Its colours were described rather obscurely as being 'similar to the Dutch but placed trans-versely instead of horizontally'. In fact it was made up of red, white and blue triangles, with the white one on the outer edge.

At the end of this first occupation the Boers set up a camp at Congella and declared Durban a magisterial district with Alexander Biggar as its first landdrost.

But it was not 'the final abandonment by Great Britain' and Napier bided his time for three years until the Boers took a decision to drive out all blacks not working for whites. The Cape Governor believed this would further destabilise the eastern Cape frontier and he ordered Captain Thomas Charlton Smith, a veteran of Waterloo, to march with a company of 263 men from the fortified post at Umazi River near Port St John's to Durban. Smith, on arrival, tore down the Boer flag at Fort Victoria. But he did not occupy it, choosing to build a new fort at his camp which is now the Old Fort. Smith attacked the Boer position at Congella on the night of 23 May 1842, but his force was repelled and, with six-pounder guns captured from the British, the Boers laid siege to him in the Old Fort.

Dick King, who was on board the trading vessel *Mazeppa* when the battle took place, was approached on 25 May by Durban trader G. C. Cato to take a message from Smith to the garrison at Fort Pedi near Grahamstown. To avoid Boer lookouts, he was ferried with his sixteen-year-old servant Ndongeni and two horses to Salisbury Island from where they followed a secret path back to the mainland. Riding 1 000 kilometres over rough, dangerous countryside during which they crossed 122 rivers, King reached Grahamstown ten days later. Reinforcements were dispatched by sea via Port Elizabeth, and they arrived in Durban between 24 and 26 June to lift the siege. On 15 July the Boers surrendered in Pietermaritzburg.

As the British extended their control over Natal, so most of the Boers again trekked. The Pretorius family headed into the interior to the Zuid-Afrikaansche Republiek (ZAR). The Boers in the region north of the Vaal River were fractious and within the claimed borders of the ZAR was a multiplicity of republics, some no bigger than a city state. When they arrived Marthinus purchased the farm Kalkheuvel near Broederstroom in the Cashan (Magaliesberg) mountains.

He loved the drama of the Highveld, the big sky which could turn from brilliant blue to brooding anger sending vicious strikes of lightning to herald shattering thunder. The land was strong and rugged, but rewarding if you bent to its demands. He loved the mountains blueing in the distance only to then be painted in blood and orange. It was not Natalia, but the bushveld had a magic of its own. From his stoep he could see the massive heads that guarded Hartbeespoort; the river cutting a welcome slash across the landscape.

The farm needed lots of work, which Marthinus was not afraid of. He rolled up his sleeves and got down to it and his father sent helpers when he could. First he built accommodation for his work-force and moved his family in with them for a time. The cattle took happily to the veld, Aletta started a vegetable garden and they ploughed a field for mielies. It had been a tough time and when it eased he was more than happy to hide in the bosom of his family and avoid being sucked into local politics.

Then his father died in 1853.

He loved his father; they had lived a dozen lives together, they shared the cold dark stars, the camp fire; they had fought shoulder to shoulder, looked death in the eye and stared it down. His father was there for him when he lost four children. They both knew death as an ever-present reminder of their destiny. He knew his father was near his maker the last time he went to Grootplaas. Yet when news reached them at Kalkheuval he was devastated. It was so final; thank the Lord his mother passed away a few years ago. The funeral was exhausting. His father had been Commandant-General of the Republic and his funeral attracted many dignitaries, each of whom felt the need say something. All the family wanted was to say their last goodbyes, but it was not to be. The Dominee and his men had to have their say.

Dominee Dirk van der Hoff approached him with a koeksuster and cup of coffee after his father's funeral service.

'Walk with me,' said the minister.

Pretorius was nervous of him; van der Hoff was at the centre of a move to break away from the Dutch Reform Church and set up a Voortrekker church. He did not want to be part of this. A little way off he found himself surrounded – there was Paul Kruger, Stephanus Schoeman, Viljoen and van Rensburg.

'This may not be the best time, but when it comes to affairs of state there are no best times,' said the Dominee. 'We want you to be the next Commandant-General.'

'Gentlemen, I do not have time for this. I'm a farmer; Paul's a soldier, choose him. I must now join my family.'

'You're a national hero, Marthinus, your country needs you,' interjected Kruger. 'You're a leader. Those families you brought from Natalia will follow you anywhere.'

'Gentlemen, we don't have a war and you don't need a Commandant-General, certainly not me.'

'Marthinus, your country needs you for bigger things. Commandant-General is a title that you'll probably never be called to use.'

He accepted the post, though it was not the hollow title they suggested. He was continuously consulted on defence, business, diplomacy, public religion, stock theft, even the purchase of coffee beans. There he showed a natural ability to handle problems at a national level, and so was forced into public life, often acting as a head of state. And he found himself enjoying the politics he had so vehemently avoided.

His dream was Boer unity, for which he strived most of the rest of his life. But the Transvaal had holes carved out of it like a round of Stilton cheese and to the south hung the Orange Free State where President Boshoff was at odds with him. After the death of his father, he moved to Potchefstroom as the last head of state of the Potchefstroom Republic; a position he held until 1856. While there, he purchased land at Elandspoort for a *kerkplaas* (church square) to serve the community around Irene. When the first whites visited in 1829, the region was occupied by Mzilikazi, a breakaway Zulu chief who founded the Matabele nation. By 1855 a town had begun developing round the church square and it was christened Pretoria Philadelphia, but later shortened to Pretoria. Five years later the capital was moved from Potchefstroom to here.

'The prettiest of the South African towns, with its red and white houses, its tall clumps of trees and pink lines of blooming rose hedges,' enthused Rider Haggard in *Jess*.

There was much general dissatisfaction in the Transvaal, which brought about a new election. Pretorius found himself standing against W. F. Joubert. Pretorius was a personable, good-looking man with remarkably blue eyes and a noble head. He was also a Trek and commando leader and national hero, so it was not surprising he was elected the first President of the Transvaal in January 1857 in a disappointingly small poll. This led to a stand-off with Stephanus Schoeman who, with the encouragement of Boshoff in the Orange Free State, elected his own Volksraad in Lydenberg and even declared war on Pretorius in April. Kruger, who was a fast-rising star, supported Pretorius and intervened with all his tact and diplomatic skills to save the day. The ZAR Constitution was redrafted, resulting in the Rustenberg Grondwet of 1858, which was accepted by the Soutspansberg, Lydenberg and Utrecht Republics in the following year. That left only the Orange Free State out of the fold, which he thought he bagged with his election victory there in 1859.

In the Orange Free State, though, Pretorius encountered more problems than he could deal with – some of his own making after he had installed a weak administration with jobs given to incompetent and invariably dishonest friends. He also inherited the running battle with Moshweshwe, his Basotho neighbour.

Pretorius complained to Moshweshwe about cattle-rustling incursions into the republic, but the monarch replied that as far as he was concerned, there was no border. He had not agreed to a border and if others had done so without him, that was their affair. Pretorius then wrote to the new Cape Governor, Philip Wodehouse, complaining that Moshweshwe was feeding on the confusion of the republic's borders.

But most of the border disputes were taking place to the west of the Orange Free State. Individual Griqua landowners between the Riet and the Orange rivers were selling their farms in this arid region to whites. Adam Kok was their chief and when Sir George Grey suggested that they move to the eastern Cape just below Basotholand, he jumped at the offer. When Pretorius became president nearly all the farms had been acquired and in 1862 what was now the District of Philippolis became a sovereign part of the Orange Free State. A few years later the richest diamond field in the world was discovered here which would have enormous implications for the future direction of Southern Africa.

Pretorius decided it was time to visit the Cape to sort matters out. At this time he was not a Freemason, but suspected his father had been. There were so many Masons who had trekked that the lodge in Graaff-Reinet had been forced to close for a while. His father had always spoken kindly of Freemasons, saying they did charity work and looked after one another. He called them a brotherhood like a commando, but was secretive about what they did, saying only that Marthinus must wait and see.

'Mr President, are you and I really going to be Freemasons?' asked Pretorius's secretary while nervously sipping his nightcap.

'Sure! You and I are going to be Masons,' replied Pretorius with a twinkle in his eye and a toast of old Cape brandy. 'Christoffel Brand was quite insistent. He said to me, "Marthinus, you must become a Freemason." So I asked, "How will that help me with Moshweshwe?" And he replied, "It won't. It'll be good for you. It's the finest organisation in the world and one every noble person should belong to. We'll try to get Wodehouse to come along."'

'What do you know about them?' the secretary pleaded.

'I don't know too much about them. I think my father was one and there were some on the Groot Trek. In Graaff-Reinet they used to parade through the streets. They did a lot of good work there, had a hospital and a rehabilitation centre for drunks. And those people we were with tonight were good people.'

'Didn't your father tell you anything?'

'Not much. Only that they were good people.'

The lamp sent amber rays through his glass.

'But...'

'What's worrying you? What can they do to us? It's not like facing a Zulu impi at Blood River.'

'Nothing. Is it because Wodehouse is one?'

'No. I think I always wanted to be a Freemason. It's funny that Wodehouse is one. That bastard thinks we're a bunch of country bumpkins. We'll show him he's no better than us. I think the old man, Christoffel Brand, can get things done. He's also a Boer, understands our psyche, and his legal standing and political position will get us a hearing. Wodehouse will listen to him. I like his son Johannes. I'd love to have him on our side. Perhaps we could persuade him to come to Bloemfontein as our Chief Justice to get the court on a proper footing. I don't believe it'll be easy though; he has so much going for him in the Cape. But he has a place in his heart for the Free State.'

'You'll have to work on him.'

'I certainly will. He knows those Englishmen; he studied there, was even called to the bar in London. He could sort them out if he put his mind to it.'

The next morning was clear as only the Cape can be. Pretorius met Bredell for breakfast then they went their separate ways – Bredell to see the Governor's secretary and he to Christoffel Brand to try and find a way to see Wodehouse. When Pretorius returned in the evening, Bredell was waiting for him in the lounge.

'Hello Carl. How was your day?' greeted Pretorius while adjusting his cravat.

'You know how it is, Mr President, our submission has been entered. It was received most courteously, but who knows what will happen next?'

'Let's see what Brand can do.'

A carriage arrived soon after to collect them. Johannes Brand was already out of the carriage, ready to help them up. Christoffel waited inside for them. Both were dressed in black with three-cornered hats. On route, Christoffel assured them that the real work would start the next day. And he had no doubt they would get an appointment with Sir Phillip Wodehouse.

The massive gates to Stahl Plein were opened and they clattered into the grounds of Lodge de Goede Hoop. They were greeted by the imperious P. G. van der Byl, the Director of Ceremonies, who introduced them to the Master and brethren, especially Jan Hendrik Hofmeyr, the deacon who would be their guide for the evening. Whilst Christoffel and Johannes went off to put on their aprons, medals and jewels, Hofmeyr led them to a little room where they were 'prepared' and left to contemplate. When he returned, he blindfolded them before leading them to the initiation ceremony presided over by Christoffel Brand.

There was so much that it was impossible to take it all in. The ceremony and lessons were delivered with flawless ease, in words that had been honed over centuries, all from memory. They were awed by the beauty of the building, but the lessons from time immemorial, dressed around ancient masons' working tools, flowed over them and diverted their attention. Addresses about their duty to the land of their birth and residence resonated in his mind. His Volksraad should hear this. He could remember a very beautiful piece delivered by Johannes Brand about the love of and respect for God's creation. After about five hours it was all over and they closed the lodge. Or so he thought.

Young Brand showed Pretorius round the building. The lodge was laid out much like a synagogue or parliament with the seats along the sides and the ceremony taking place in the middle. The walls were lined with the most beautiful statues by Anton Anreith and he was fascinated by the framed original drawings by Thibault in the foyer. They then sent for him to inform him that the Council had decided to make him an Honorary Past Master, which was an incredible honour.

Pretorius got to see Wodehouse, but as Theal records, 'the intercourse between Sir Philip and the President was unfriendly from the start so he got nowhere.' He also met with Johannes Brand and discussed the establishment of a supreme court, but this came to nothing as the republic did not have the funds to finance it. But the trip was not a complete failure: he had become a Freemason and, though he did not know it at the time, had opened the door for Johannes to become President of the Orange Free State.

When Pretorius got back to Bloemfontein he became aware that the English were in the process of forming a lodge. Not to be out-done, he petitioned Sir Christoffel Brand, Deputy Grand Master National GEN, to form a lodge the following year. Pretorius was not deterred by a lack of members as he coerced English Masons who were trying to form their own lodge to join his petitioners. As a result, Lodge Unie (Union) was consecrated on 15 October 1864. He bullied eleven men into initiation, including J. C. Nielen Marais and A. B. Roberts from his government.

But the Free Staters were becoming disillusioned by his inability to come to terms with Moshweshwe, his poor administration and his commuting between the two republics. He was also unable to unite the Boer people, who were used to governing themselves and would not submit to central government. Leading the campaign against him was, of all people, the Master of the lodge he had started, H. A. L. Hamelberg, the outspoken owner of *De Tijd* news-paper. He wrote, 'Our President is more interested in a willow tree on his farm in the Transvaal, than our state.' Pretorius resigned. Then the Free Staters got cold feet and begged him to stay, which he did. In an about-face they fired him a few months later and he left with a heavy heart. In one last cast of the die he proposed Johannes Brand as a candidate for president and was a little sur-prised when the Volksraad accepted the nomination.

While Pretorius was trying to sort out the Free State there were interesting things going on in the Transvaal. The Volksraad started to take Sir George Grey's warning more seriously and with the problems in Bloemfontein asked Pretorius to step aside. Stephanus Schoeman assumed the presidency of the Transvaal, arguing that he was the 'senior president' as he was president of the Lydenburg Republic long before the other contenders were president of anything. Then Paul Kruger threw him out. It was suggested at the time that Kruger should himself take over, but he felt he was too young and put van Rensburg into the job. Before he could take office, though, Viljoen arrived and took over. This prompted Kruger to call an election and in a turn-up, Pretorius's old enemy Schoeman begged him to stand. Van Rensburg won, but the poll was annulled. Then came a new election, which van Rensberg won as well. This nearly resulted in civil war and another poll was called, which Pretorius won.

Pretorius remained in office for seven years. Much time was spent sorting out the mess, which, to be fair, he had a hand in creating. Like the leopard, he could not change his spots and in December 1867 it was rumoured that gold was discovered in East Matabeleland. He dashed off and annexed the land, which for a brief time gave him an outlet to the sea, but the Portuguese and the British took it back. His time was also marked by continuous raids against the Pedi and a clash with Brand. He eventually resigned the presidency and retired from public life. He was succeeded by Thomas Francis Burgers, also a Freemason, who gave him a number of government commissions to occupy himself until he died in 1901.

Pretorius was a man of passion and fervour for his country. He seemed insensitive to insults and rebuffs and was a headstrong opportunist easily misled. Unfortunately he was never the statesman everyone hoped he would become.

Chapter 10
Johannes Hendricus Brand

Brand was the right man at the right time for the Free State. The Afrikaner was at the beginning of his cultural and political development... One of the negative results of the Trek was that its people did not advance in a cultural sense. The conditions under which the Voortrekker leaders were chosen did not require that they be men of education... military ability and strong personality-yes!... but their limitations were felt only when the time came to establish a government. To rescue these states, it was necessary for the Afrikaner to find amongst his own people the men who could take on the almost superhuman job. No outsider could do it... With Brand's coming, the Free State reached the turning point towards stability.

– G. D. Scholtz

The open carriage slowly made its way down Charles Street, which was lined with people waving any orange thing they could lay their hands on. Hamelberg made him wear this orange sash like the ones over the khaki uniforms of the mounted Boers who escorted him to the new cathedral. The animation they brought to the parade was just outweighed by the dust they created when the procession crossed the market square. A bead of sweat found its way out from under the black silk Bell Topper hat he was expected to wear and ran down his face.

He felt only marginally rested after the last few, hectic days. He had arrived in Bloemfontein on Saturday 29 November 1863. He and the family had come by train to Philippolis and from there they took a leisurely carriage ride to the capital, stopping on the way to greet people who turned out in their droves, and overnighted at Trompsberg, Edenburg and Reddersburg. They were welcomed wherever they stopped, with Bloemfontein excelling itself. A large part of the population left home on horseback, in carts, wagons and all sorts of other vehicles at four in the morning to meet them at Kaffir Kop some four miles outside town. The whole party drew up in line to receive them and a volley of small arms was fired as a salute. Sabilia was miffed when Brand was asked to ride in the secretary's carriage for the last part of the journey, consoling herself with the thought that they needed to brief him about something or other. He would tell her tonight.

They reached Bloemfontein at three in the afternoon where he was addressed by the municipal commissioner, to which he responded orally. The next night there was a banquet attended by seventy gentlemen, who all said the same thing – things were bad, they needed to get their produce to the coast, they wanted to get a railway line connected to Cape Town, they wanted jobs and industry, and he was the one to do it for them.

The crowds were becoming thicker as they got closer to the church; he picked out more individuals in the crowd, smiled and waved at them. The carriage drew to a halt; the escort jumped off their horses and were looking for a place to tie them up somewhere behind the crowd while he sat in the sun. Eventually they assembled in two columns and only then would they allow him off. Now he had to meet the dignitaries; he knew Hamelberg, Barlow, Orpen and de Waal, but none of the others. Finally they marched him into the dark cool of the church, rainbows flashed behind his eyelids as he got used to the darkness.

Sabilia was waiting for him in the front row, just like at their wedding. Everyone thought he was crazy to give up a career in England for her; he might have been a judge by now, but then being a president was not exactly a failure. He was in love with her then, just as much as he was in love with her now, and would do it all over again. He put out his hand and she took it just as she did all those years ago. The priest and other dignitaries were confused as this was not in the script, but they would just have to get used to the fact that he did things his way. They took him to a seat and found one for Sabilia on the stage. He rather hoped Pretorius would come; after all it was he who started it all, but he was not there. He could hardly blame him. He watched the fan go round and round, finding it difficult to concentrate on Hamelberg, who was explaining to the congregants how presidents of the Orange Free State were elected.

In this particular election there were four candidates: J. J. Venter, Joseph Allison, M. Bowker and Johannes Brand. He then went on to tell how Brand's name got onto the list. 'You know that he was nearly our Chief Justice and for no fault of his own it fell through. I want to read from a letter he wrote to us at that the time: "I believe the Free State presents me with great opportunities to promote the welfare of my countrymen, in which I take the deepest interest... impartially to administer justice and to train young people in the law. I have come to the conclusion that the Free State has strong claims upon me."'

'Even then I knew he was the man for us,' continued Hamelberg. 'You know that we in the Free State have no party politics so he had to canvas on his own and to do that from Cape Town was difficult. He was thus hesitant to accept a nomination, but did and said this at his farewell dinner: "My future lot, I feel confidently, will be cast in the Free State. It was not without long and anxious consideration that I determined upon the step which I am about to take. I did not hastily come to that conclusion. Long and anxious did I deliberate. I felt it my beholden duty to await the result of the poll and if I was returned by a large majority no longer to hesitate, but regardless of the sacrifices I had to make in leaving my friends and relations I will endeavour to contribute something to the prosperity and happiness of my countrymen in the Free State." He needn't have worried as he attained the overwhelming support of the people with almost double the number of votes of the other three candidates together. Now we'll give him an Executive Council so that he can propose legislation even though he cannot vote on it.'

Raising an imaginary glass to Brand, he concluded, 'We wish him health and strength; heaven knows he'll need it as he has to tour the whole Free State once a year. So you can all look forward to a visit from our president.'

There was a giggle here and there as Hamelberg smiled at Brand and sat down. The Dominee and judge stepped forward and nudged a Bible into Brand's hands, 'Do you, Johannes Hendricus Brand, before the great God of the universe and those here present accept the office of President of the Orange Free State of you own free will and accord?'

'So help me God.'

The next few days were a thinly disguised tug-of-war between opposing parties trying to get Brand on one side or the other. The first morning kicked off with a meeting with his Executive Council followed by lunch. He had his doubts about them; many were Pretorius's cronies picked because they were yes-men. Two of them at drinks before lunch suggested he would be an asset on the board of their company. His father had advised him to bide his time before taking any action, but his goal was to assemble the best people around him.

That evening's activities were at Lodge Unie, which was special to him as it was founded by Pretorius after being initiated in Cape Town and was consecrated by his father. There was an installation of the new Master on the summons, which was a joyous working of time-honoured rituals. The banquet that followed was a delight and in a speech he told how much he owed to Freemasonry. In it he said: 'Worshipful Master, your promotion to the chair of this lodge is the greatest honour the brethren of the lodge have in their power to confer on anyone. It is also the greatest lesson in life you'll ever have. As Master of the lodge you must learn how to lead with no power. You can't fire anyone; you have no bonuses to give; and no incentives nor big sticks to wield – a bit like being president.'

That brought a little ripple of laughter.

'All you can do is to lead by example, to create a dream worth being followed by others, to inspire with your enthusiasm, be strong enough not to show disappointment, carry the weak in your wake and make them look strong. As a Freemason you must be strong in your own principles and defend them to the hilt even if unpleasant; do not bend in the pursuit of popularity; look to the Great Architect for guidance. To you younger Masons I wish to tell you that I have derived so much pleasure out of my Masonry. I joined when I was 19 years old and threw myself into it. I took on every job that came my way and I know I got more out of it than it than it than I put in. All my family have been Masons. You know my father is the Grand Master National, my grandfather was a member and my great-grandfather was a founder member of Lodge de Goede Hoop. My uncle and I have all been Masters of Lodge de Goede Hoop and I know if you apply yourselves you too will reach that high office. I am grateful to the lodge for my education; without them I could never have studied in Leyden. I have made so many lasting friendships and so will you.'

The next day the farmers and the schools wanted to know what he could provide them.

'Where do I start?'

'At the beginning,' said Sabilia, wiping her hands on her apron. 'There's so much to do.'

'Go and find good men you can trust, bring some from Cape Town if you must.'

'I know nothing of business. How can I fix that?'

'Get someone who does. What about that nice Jewish man with the holiday home in Summerstrand?'

'Leviseur? Then there's Hamelberg who is a man of many talents and honest.' Hamelberg was probably the only honest one from the last administration, which the *Friend* newspaper referred to as a 'paradise of fools'.

During his first term, Brand weeded out the incompetent and corrupt, with one landing in jail and others running off to the Transvaal. He brought in anyone who was competent, be they English or Boer, Christian or Jew, and won the trust of the Volksraad. His first term he spent bringing peace and unity, but he was still criticised by the *Friend* for having let the economy and internal administration slip. This was a little unfair because he had scarcely got to Bloemfontein when trouble flared again with Moshweshwe. Despite all this, he agreed to stand for a second term only if he received support from a majority of the population, which he did.

⎯⎯•⎯⎯

'Brand, my dear fellow, how are you?' greeted Wodehouse, shaking his hand and looking deeply into his eyes.

'Very well, thank you, Sir Philip. I must thank you most sincerely for coming to collect us in your carriage at the station yesterday'

'Think nothing of it, my dear fellow. I'm only sorry that you're not staying with us here at Government House or at the guesthouse.'

'My father would not hear of it. To you I may be a head of state; to him I'm still his child. He still tells me how to dress and corrects me when I talk.'

'Aha!' snorted Wodehouse. 'How are you settling down in Bloemfontein? I hear through the grapevine that you've done some spring-cleaning there.'

Brand explained how he had to weed out the bad apples in his administration, deal with a crook or two, and form a proper management team. No sooner was that done than troubles with Moshweshwe started all over again.

'This was after you were kind enough to assist in our negotiations with Moshweshwe in setting the boundary,' said Brand. 'I really believed that it was the end of the matter.'

'I've heard that he's up to his old tricks.'

'I think Moshweshwe would have respected the boundary, but he's an old man and losing control. There's a struggle for power back home; his son Molapo and his nephew Lesaona would not agree to the delineation. They continued with the raids on our farms and, as you know, my people will not stand by and let it happen. They have a long history of looking after themselves and taking the law into their own hands. I had to call out the national commando on 9 June 1865.'

'I know about that. I'm told you played a personal role in that,' smiled Wodehouse.

'It's been said that the Boer is one of the finest soldiers the world has ever seen – can shoot a coin out of the sky. But they're farmers, they love the soil, you see them feeling it, even when they're sitting in the veld with their coffee. The smallest rumour of trouble at home and you hear the call "*huis toe*" (Let's go home). Now, you know I am no soldier; hell, I can't hit a coin if you put it on top of the rifle. But I know my people and I set up my own camp, lit my own fire and tended my own coffee pot and told them stories of the Cape. They know very little about the world and they lapped it up, which provides the opportunity to weave in little inspirational dreams.'

'They tell me you have this saying of yours: *alles zal reg kommen.*'

'Everything will be alright,' translated Brand. 'We drove them out of the Caledon River valley back into their mountain homeland. They capitulated and accepted terms, harsh ones, 3 000 head of cattle and all the territory under dispute.'

Wodehouse's eyebrows shot up, 'Harsh, I'll say.'

'Well, I think they stole about that number of cattle. I would not let my men take more.'

'But the whole valley?'

'I think your predecessors clouded the question of the border. Sir George Napier tried to set it in 1843; Sir Harry Smith wanted each side to keep what they had and to stop fighting; then Warden gave Moshweshwe ground that we believe was ours. Now they have started yet again. To prevent us retaliating they've submitted themselves to your protection.'

'Any aggression against them would be one against Her Majesty.'

'I'm sensitive to that issue. That's why I'm here. I brought Hamelberg, Barlow and Orpen along, but I am grateful that we could meet like this first. Phillip, I'll not be able to stop my people from retrieving what's rightfully theirs no matter what anyone thinks. You must understand that the Orange Free State is a complex society. The southerners ally themselves with the Cape and the northerners with Transvaal. If you don't act with an eye to justice you'll split them and the Orange Free State. The Transvaal will happily take the northerners and join them in an action against you and the Basothos. The southerners will drift towards the Cape: not the western Cape, but the eastern Cape who are already talking of breaking away.'

'Don't think I am unaware of these issues,' said Wodehouse, resting his chin on his tented fingers. 'Johannes, you know I hold your father in high regard. He's the speaker of my House of Assembly. And you cannot be insensitive to the fact that I have a high regard for you personally, but I'll have to stop any raids into Basutoland.'

'And what about the other way round?' challenged Brand.

'Well, you know I'll do everything I can. But I have strict instructions from Her Majesty's—'

'Phillip, all my energies in the short time I've been in the hot seat are to show my people that they can and will succeed as a nation. Sadly, you and I are set on paths that that will collide. I cannot allow criminal elements in Basutoland to rip my nation apart.'

'Things may not be as clear-cut as you put them. I don't have the final say.'

'Phillip, you and I will take the fall if you plunge us into a war.'

'Steady on, old chap.'

'Let your people meet mine; go through their papers and let them present to you. Or arrange a negotiation forum, or an open debate; we'll do it any way that suits you.'

The Orange Free State made a powerful case, won themselves clear boundaries, and secured peace through the Second Treaty of Aliwal North in February 1869.

Brand loved children and knew they liked him. Since arriving in Bloemfontein he had played this little game: whenever he passed youngsters in the street he would lift his hat with old-time manners and say 'Good morning, ladies or gentlemen' and walk on. They would titter and squeal behind his back, which always brought a smile to his lips even though he pretended not to notice. He was a devoted father and husband, writing to his children advising, as any loving father might, 'Take every advantage of your education opportunities; it is all I can give you, don't borrow money, keep your bowels open.'

When he first came to the Orange Free State there were hardly any schools. He had teaching in his blood and brought teachers from Cape Town and Port Elizabeth and they travelled all over the state, founding schools in every town and village. Where there were no facilities he commandeered churches, even shops, and sometimes a big tree. Brand presented himself at examinations to encourage students, and when he visited schools he would give them all a holiday so they could sit in the playground and chat.

'Give everyone the respect they deserve and always remember a Free Stater has good manners, is considerate and kind,' he always told them.

⸻ • ⸻

No sooner had Brand signed the treaty with Moshweshwe than he faced problems on another border. Diamonds were discovered in Kimberley, eight kilometres within the Orange Free State. As Patrick Hopkins writes:

> From each port and lowly dorp
> From Land's End to Zanzibar
> Men came to the land of promise
> Weaving dreams of sparkling splendour.
> From rush to rush to peg a claim
> And lose, then peg again.
>   – Unknown

In 1866 near Hopetown, a farmer's wife noticed that one of the pretty stones her children had picked up on the riverbank and were playing with in the yard had an unusual sparkle in the bright sunlight. She presented it to Schalk van Niekerk, a neighbouring farmer and family friend, who sent it for assessment. The stone was declared to be a twenty-one-carat diamond worth £500.

The stone attracted little further interest, but it gave van Niekerk an element of local renown for his savvy in realising it might have some value – a reputation that brought a Griqua shepherd bearing a superb white diamond to him in March 1869. Van Niekerk, on seeing the stone, offered the shepherd his entire livestock of 500 sheep, ten oxen and a horse. The farmer then sold the 83-carat diamond – to become known as the Star of South Africa – to a dealer for £11 200 who, in turn, sold it to a London company for £25 000. More than that, however, it unleashed a frenzy seldom seen before or since.

The rush was on and diggers converged on Hopetown and the banks of the Vaal River – the few who struck it lucky enough to drink champagne and light cigars with banknotes driving the rest in this ultimate of gambles. Ragged prospect towns such as Austin's Rush, Poorman's Koppie, Moonlight Rush, Gong Gong, Longlands and Sydney-on-Vaal quickly sprang up on the sun-blasted landscape. They were all much of a muchness – weather-discoloured tents interspersed with trading stores and many bars, concert halls, shooting galleries, billiard saloons and gambling dens. In fact, places of ill repute were so numerous in Hebron alone that it was forced to relinquish its biblical name for the more prosaic Windsorton.

Then came the significant finds in Griqualand West, near the Vaal River, on the farms Bultfontein, Dorstfontein (Dutoitspan) and Vooruitzicht. On a nearby hillock, Colesberg Kopje, the richest treasure house of all was found. This brought another 50 000 hopefuls from around the world. Fortune seekers and adventurers left their homes in Europe, the United States, Australia, Asia and South America; others jumped ship or deserted armies. The grey, dusty air round the Kimberley camp was soon filled with the noise of soil-sifting cradles being rocked, shouted orders, metal clanging on rocks, squeaking barrows, hype, honky-tonk and the buzz of flies.

Brand sent O. J. Truter and J. B. Robinson to administer the diamond fields, which by all accounts they did very well. Now everyone wanted them – and for good reason. Sir Richard Southey, District Grand Master and Governor of the Cape, made a challenge for them, feeling Britain had a claim as protector of the people.

'Gentlemen,' he prophesised to the Cape assembly while holding up the Hope Diamond, 'this is the rock on which the future success of South Africa will be built.'

David Arnot, Brand's old school friend, had qualified as a lawyer with a reputation for being sharp to the point of dishonesty. He persuaded Griqua chief Waterboer to lay claim to the diamond fields. His reward for a successful outcome was thirteen farms. Adam Kok was mystified that it was not his, and Marthinus Pretorius also laid claim on the basis of them being north of the Vaal. And it was he who had bought them while president of the Orange Free State.

The British, being the dominant force in the region, arranged for arbitration. Brand called for an international arbitrator while the British prevailed with their own man, Keate, from Natal. Brand, therefore, would have nothing to do with the process. Pretorius decided that he and his state attorney would present the Transvaal case, but their submission was extremely incompetent as they did not prepare the witnesses or their evidence at all. They only produced a document dated 1851, ostensibly proving their ownership of the ground, but the watermark showed 1868. Arnot, on the other hand, was brilliant and by the time he had finished with them the Transvaal had not only lost their claim, but a portion of their own country. This debacle led to the resignation of Pretorius as president of the Transvaal and in an amazing turnabout Brand was offered the position, but he declined and recommended a fellow Freemason, T. F. Burgers, who was elected.

Southey was determined that the diamond fields would remain under British control and got up to every shady trick to ensure this would happen. He invited Waterboer and his people to become British citizens; he even had the boundaries resurveyed using incorrect information so that the site of what was later to become Kimberley fell outside the borders of the Orange Free State. The original boundaries of 1838 were set by natural features; in this case a line between a point on the Modder River called David's Grave and a mountain called Platkop (flat head). But almost all the mountains there have flat heads and it was only too easy to find one that suited him.

Southey wrote this shameful letter to London:

> If by our taking over, Arnot retains title to the lands Waterboer has given him, he will be a lucky man; and if Waterboer and his subjects retain their lands or get value for what is disposed of to private individuals then he will also be fortunate. We cannot take all the chestnuts out of the fire and get none for ourselves after they are out.

By no stretch of the imagination could this be called fair or just. The Orange Free State had bought the ground and if there was something wrong with the transaction then presumably Adam Kok would have a claim; Waterboer never wanted it and made no move to use or occupy it but the dominant force at the time wanted it and would stop at nothing to get it.

The arbitration was held with Keate as arbitrator. Waterboer was awarded the territory, Arnot got his farms, and the Griqua became British subjects. A bolder Waterboer, encouraged by new friends, wanted more. This time Colonel Charles Warren, the first Master of Quatuor Coronati Lodge and a frequent visitor to Rising Star Lodge in Bloemfontien, was the arbitrator. He dismissed Waterboer's claim and told him to be content with what he received at the first arbitration.

During the dispute, Brand sent Hamelberg to see Lord Kimberley in London, but he was led on a wild goose chase and saw nobody. Finally Brand went to England and met with the Secretary of State for the Colonies, Lord Carnarvon, who was also Deputy Grand Master of England, and the matter was settled to Brand's satisfaction; or so he telegraphed Bloemfontien. The arbitration ruling would stand as set out previously, but the Orange Free State would be compensated £90 000 for their loss. Many believed that Brand had lost and was sent on his way with a not-so-golden-handshake but Sophie Leviseur put it in perspective with these words: 'That £90 000 was really the foundation of the prosperity of the Free State.' The sum represented sufficient capital to start a national bank. Brand also won postal privileges and a railway extension to Bloemfontein.

———▸•◂———

'Francis! Come give me a hug,' Brand heard Sabilia call out. With an arm round him she brought him into the kitchen.

'Mr President, it's indeed a pleasure being here,' grinned Reitz.

Brand rose and shook his hand while holding onto his elbow. He was trying to hide his emotions while directing Reitz onto a *riempie* chair at the scrubbed oak table.

'I think I always knew you and I would work together some day,' smiled Brand. 'As long ago as that night you were initiated with Melius de Villiers in Lodge de Goede Hoop.'

'I never saw it, what with all the arguments and disagreements we had when I was your student.'

'Add those two pictures together and you'll see why. I knew. What has happened to Schriener?'

'Well, you know he's now my brother-in-law.'

'I heard. That's why I ask. The two of you were a handful,' laughed Brand. 'Tell me what's happening in the lodge.'

In 1864 Johannes Andreas Truter was installed as Master. He was the grandson of Sir John Truter and his father O. J. Truter had been recently made Acting Deputy Grand Master. Southey, Provincial Grand Master for South Africa under the Grand Lodge of England, visited the lodge on 24 June 1865. In the same year two American men-o-war, the corvette *Wachusetts* and the frigate *Hartford*, arrived in Cape Town and eight of their complement were initiated. At the time there was an average of nine meetings a month and in 1866 J. A. Truter was re-elected. At one of these meetings six candidates were initiated, representing a group so worthy that it is unlikely ever to have been repeated anywhere in the world. They were: Andries Stockenström, son of the past Governor, who would become a judge and Provincial Grand Master; Advocate John Henry de Villiers (later first Lord de Villiers), who would become Chief Justice of the Cape, Chief Justice of South Africa, president of the National Convention and Provincial Grand Master; Dr Antonio Lorenzo Chiappini; Advocate (later Sir) John Buchanan, who would become Judge President of Griqualand West, Judge of the Supreme Court and Acting Chief Justice of the Cape; and Jan Hendrik Hofmeyr, son of the Master of the Supreme Court and Deputy Grand Master.

'Oh! This will interest you,' said Reitz. 'They created a new form of member somewhere between an effective member and a non-member, called a working member.'

'That sounds like a good move,' said Brand as Sabilia brought in coffee.

Brand had agonised over Reitz. He knew he was brilliant and just the right man to help him with the Supreme Court and drafting the county's constitution. He would be an excellent Chief Justice. He first made overtures to Johan de Villiers, but he had committed himself to the Cape. Whereas he never doubted Reitz's brilliance, he was concerned by his passion for side issues like poetry, writing in the colloquial and his affiliation with the Afrikanerbond. He was also headstrong, his own man and, at thirty, too young. On Hamelberg's advice, he got the Volksraad to agree to his appointment, but he would have to keep a tight rein on him.

They worked well together and the Constitutions of both the Orange Free State and the Supreme Court were put in place. Bryce called the Constitution, 'the finest constitution for the government of civilised men.' The Supreme Court they established still functions today as the seat of the South African Appeal Court.

His father, Sir Christoffel Brand, died on 19 May 1875, nine months after retiring. Johannes Brand's whole family as well as Lodge de Goede Hoop attended the funeral on 31 May. A Lodge of Sorrows was held and a three-month mourning period was declared by the lodge. A move was made to erect a memorial to him, but there is no record of what was eventually done.

Numerous things were said at the various services and those that stuck in Brand's mind were: Outside of Freemasonry,

> Sir Christoffel is best known as the first Speaker of the Parliament of the colony of the Cape of Good Hope, an office he held from 1854 to 1874, when his failing health forced him to retire. There can be no doubt that his influence greatly contributed to the dignity and order of the House of Assembly: as a competent observer said when he had been two years in office, 'This Speaker's conduct in the Chair has done much to maintain the dignity of the House'.

As to his Masonic career, the *South African Record* says,

> An ardent, an enthusiastic, and conscientious Mason. Despite his numerous avocations, he was always ready and willing to assist other constitutions whenever his aid or advice was sought. His best Masonic abilities, and they were many and great, were ever at the service of his brethren of the craft and he was frequently requested to act as arbitrator in Masonic disputes, and to unravel knotty tangles in regard to Masonic law and procedure. He was in all respects a genuine Masonic diplomat; and among the members of his own Constitution he was indeed set as a terror to evildoers and praise of them that did well.

Although Brand had kept up his association with Lodge de Goede Hoop, the visit to Cape Town gave him an opportunity to catch up with his friends. The major change since he had left for the Orange Free State was the slide from Dutch to English, which caused some dissent. As far back as 1855 they began introducing English rituals to stem the loss of English members. This was followed by a new translation of Dutch rituals into English and by 1870 English was being used in minutes and transactions.

On St John's Day in June 1872 the orator, Brother Reverend D. P. Faure (Truter's son-in-law), proposed transactions expressing thankfulness for the end of the Franco-Prussian war and stated that disputes between nations should be settled by peaceful means. Christoffel Brand used the occasion to install his successor. This had been opposed, but Brand cited ill-health as the reason. In the same year he got all the lodges together to celebrate South African Freemasonry's centenary.

'Hell, do you remember the debate about the date?' reminisced Dirk van Breda. 'As the warrant states the first day of the ninth month was September, but de Mist had said it was November.'

'So they went with him,' said John Buchanan.

'It was a most remarkable festival attended by more than 200 Masons, including the Deputy Grand Master your father, the Provincial Grand Master Brother J. H. de Villiers, Southey and his deputy Sir Thomas Maclear,' continued van Breda. 'The Master welcomed the honoured guests and the orator spoke on larger issues. We then enjoyed a splendid banquet, which included toasts to the Queen and replies from the Governor.'

On his return to Bloemfontein, Brand appointed Hamelberg as his representative to get the Orange Free State international recognition. The Cape and Transvaal regarded the Free State as a part of their influence and he wanted to reduce reliance on his neighbours. Hamelberg started with Holland where Brand's friend Professor Johan Rudolf Thorbecke was prime minister. He also got in contact with another of Brand's university friends, John Louden, who was Governor-General of the Dutch East Indies.

The Orange Free State sent a display to the Philadelphia Exhibition in 1876, which was described as 'a highly creditable display for so young a state'. At the same time Hamelberg worked on the United States. The relationship with England was good after the diamond fiasco and ties were established with Italy and France, but Germany was left for a while as they were too close to Kruger in the Transvaal.

Brand also began focusing on moving the Orange Free State away from its agrarian roots. He needed to create jobs as there was a negative social impact from many of the population working in Kimberley. His beloved lodge could scarcely open because most of the men were there. He was convinced that if there were minerals so close to his border there must be in his country as well. He employed a geologist from Kimberley, George William Stowe, who found the northern coal fields and even suggested oil might be found, but he missed the very rich gold fields altogether. He kept England to its promise and the postal system was brought up to date and expanded and a bridge was built over the Orange River. And with Reitz's help he encouraged farmers to experiment with tobacco and wool, which enjoyed moderate success.

Brand became ill with Bright's disease towards the latter half of his second term and even thought of vacating the presidency. He recovered and was persuaded to stand for a third term in which he was re-elected after polling 27 of the 38 delegates. Freemasonry was always important to him and having Reitz, Hamelberg, Orpen and many other Masons around him made it more meaningful. It was a thread that ran through his life and though he could not spend as much time as he would like on it he was nevertheless the father figure they all looked up to. He resolved their difficulties and squabbles with wisdom, which is typified by the following story.

The two lodges in Bloemfontien both met on the same night and neither was prepared to change; clearly a silly thing because the members could not visit one another because they were worried they would lose members to the other. Neither would give way. We read in the minutes of Lodge Rising Star: 'There was a knock on the lodge door, which was answered by the Inner Guard who reported that the President, Master Wardens and Brethren of Lodge Unie were outside the door and respectfully request admission. The lodge discussed the matter and agreed to their request.' From then on the two lodges worked together in peace and harmony.

It was this ability to sort out issues that Brand came to be regarded as a regional statesman and he was consulted on many issues, especially those pertaining to the Boers. Barlow said of him that he was 'probably the wisest and ablest statesman South Africa has ever produced.' The Transvaal in the 1870s was an administrative mess which was having an impact beyond its borders. In 1876 the Native Administrator in Natal, Theophilus Shepstone, was instructed to annex it, which he did in 1877 with twenty-nine policemen. This led to the start of first Anglo-Boer War (known by the Boers as the War of Independence) on 16 December 1880. After a number of battles, the combatants met at Majuba Hill on 27 February 1881.

The British commander, Major-General Sir George Colley, had the previous day occupied the summit of the hill presumably to outflank the Boer positions at Laing's Nek. Nearly half his men were from the 92nd (Gordon) Highlanders. Colley, who until then was highly regarded, took no artillery with him nor did he ask his troops to dig in. While he assumed the Boers would disperse when they became aware of his position, made abundantly clear by Highlanders shouting and waving their fists, they instead organised a storming party led by Nicolas Smit.

Smit, for the first time in warfare, employed the fire and movement tactic to keep the British at bay while his three attack groups got into position. Just after midnight they reached the summit and engaged the enemy with tremendous fire while avoiding hand-to-hand combat. In panic, the surviving British fell into disarray and fled down the hill, where many more were killed, injured or captured. They tried to mount a rearguard action but this had little impact.

It was a great military blunder and the British signed a truce on 6 March and a peace treaty two weeks later. Brand had been asked by the Transvaal to provide military support, but declined. After the peace Brand was instrumental in getting the parties together, which paved the way for the signing of the Pretoria Convention on 3 May 1881 in which sovereignty was restored to the Transvaal. It is probably this that earned him a knighthood. For Brand this was a prickly issue: his mentor John Truter and his father accepted knighthoods, but they lived in a British colony. In the Orange Free State accepting the honour would not be universally welcomed.

'*Liefie*, what do you think?' enquired Brand of his wife as he leaned back in his big leather chair.

He still did not feel at home in the new residency which Hamelberg forced him to occupy. He liked the thought of conducting affairs of state in his kitchen; people were more at ease.

'Johannes, I don't know. You and I are not a "Sir and Lady". Where did all of this come from?' asked Sabilia, opening windows to let out the smell of tobacco.

'This fellow, Sir Charles Dilke, proposed the knighthood. I don't really know him, except he was tipped to become prime minister of England until it was revealed he was having an affair with a Mrs Donald Crawford. I secretly suspect Carnarvon has a hand in it.'

'What did you do for them?'

'The word is that it's for sorting out the peace settlement between the Transvaal and England.'

'Don't you think this is some sort of trap to get you on to their side?'

Before he could respond his secretary announce that Reitz, Hamelberg and Leviseur were in the study and Brand went to join them.

'Gentlemen, what are we going to do about this?' asked Brand.

'I think that to accept this would be a mistake and might destroy the great legacy you have built,' said Reitz. 'As a member of the Dutch Reformed Church you can't also be an Honorary Grand Cross of the Order of St Michael and St George.

Brand looked at Hamelberg who was becoming extremely frail, but had not lost any of the sharpness of his mind.

'I don't need to tell you how fickle politics is,' said Hamelberg. 'And as a lawyer you know that things are not always what they seem. You have walked in elevated circles so I believe you will not be out of place with that status.'

Reitz was becoming more and more agitated, 'You are a Boer first and foremost and we don't accept handouts from the enemy!'

'I don't believe we have any enemies,' whispered Brand huskily. 'I'm motivated by one thing and one thing only: what is good for my country.'

'As I was saying,' continued Hamelberg, 'I believe our countrymen know that and will accept what you decide is for the best. Why not put it to the Volksraad?'

Leviseur shuffled before speaking, 'My daughter Sophie says our other presidents were good, honest men, but not shining lights. President Pretorius did nothing for us and it was only when you became president that we made any strides forward. You established the integrity of the civil service, coordinated our laws and built wisely so that in the twenty-five years of our existence we've become a model republic. You've given us stability and built a republic we can be proud of.'

'He's right,' added Hamelberg. 'Some of our people feel close to the Cape while others favour the Transvaal. We must be ourselves and not endanger our republic.'

'Exactly,' said Reitz. 'By taking this rank you would side with the English and alienate the Boers.'

'Hamelberg, you got us accredited with England,' said Brand. 'What will it mean if we turn down their kindness?'

'The same if Holland wanted to make you a Ruiter or the French a Chevalier. Your father accepted a knighthood: what would he think if you turned it down? Would he have seen it as criticism?'

'He would say "Do your duty",' responded Brand.

'What is your duty?' asked Sabilia as she brought in coffee.

'In all truth, I simply don't know what to do,' replied Brand. 'Turning to other matters, there's a fifth term coming up. I'd rather someone else took over the reins, but the Volksraad seems determined I should carry on. The economy is in good shape, we are stable, comfortable with our neighbours, and our people are at peace with one another. When I was last in London Carnarvon planted a seed of establishing a federation of southern African states. We run our countries independently, but have a body controlling overall cooperation. I've become enamoured with the thought and Carnarvon thinks I'm the only one who can swing it. I'm not sure I can live up to his expectations, but I'm ready to try. I've invited Kruger to Bloemfontein next year to see how he feels about it. I don't think a knighthood will impress him much, but it will establish credibility with Natal and the Cape as well as the Protectorates.'

'I agree,' said Hamelberg as Reitz shook his head sadly.

'I'm going to put it to the Volksraad for them to decide,' Brand said finally, rising to indicate the meeting was over. Reitz tried to make a dash, but Brand put a hand on his arm, 'Francis, can you give me a minute or two?'

When the others had left he said to Reitz, 'I don't want a fifth term, but it looks like it will come about. There'll certainly be no sixth term. There is only one man who can take over and that's you. I have great admiration for you and have always thought you brilliant. You're like a son to me. But I want you to be a president to the whole population. I know you would like to be closer to Kruger, but I would caution against that as it can only lead to trouble; perhaps war. He believes that it is the only solution. I also know you are passionate about our culture and we must preserve it. Your Afrikanerbond has a place, but you shouldn't be running it. Both Kruger and I were angry when as my secretary of state you headed an uninvited delegation to the Paardekraal gathering in another country.'

The Volksraad voted in favour of Brand accepting the knighthood, which enhanced his image. However, some, including Reitz, thought it was his only serious mistake.

<hr>

Brand had the Masonic virtue of never holding a grudge. In about 1885 Sir Charles Warren arrived in Bloemfontein. He was the man who had ruled against the Orange Free State in the diamond fields dispute, but was welcomed not only as an old friend but as a brother.

'Come in, Sir Charles. It is such a delight to welcome you to our home,' greeted Brand. 'Sabilia insists that we sit in the front room even though I'd prefer the kitchen. A drink?'

'Yes, that would be nice. Whisky. Do you get to lodge much, Mr President?'

'Regrettably no. I try to get to all the installations of the Masters and their officers as it helps me keep in touch. I also try to get to all the special meetings.'

'Were you made a Mason while in England?' asked Warren.

'No, my father would have killed me. Tell me about your Masonry.'

'I don't get to lodge that much either. After my stint here I was sent on that Bechuanaland Expedition, then I did some excavating in Jerusalem, then they sent me to Suakin, an awful little port on the Red Sea in Sudan. Now I have been recalled to London to reorganise the London Police Force. But you know that I've been anxious for many years to form a lodge for research only and you'll be pleased to know that it's now all systems go. The Prince of Wales on 28 November 1884 issued us with a warrant for the formation of the new lodge, the Quatuor Coronati Lodge, so while organising the police I'll have more time to organise Masonic research and do a bit of visiting.'

A clatter of hooves stopped their conversation.

'That'll be the carriage,' said Brand. 'Let's go to Lodge Unie.'

Warren, after the visit, wrote of Brand, 'The President has some difficult people to deal with in the Volksraad, but he manages them so skilfully that they respect him. Though they do accuse him now and then of being too English, I think they are rather proud of him.'

⬥

Brand's last communication was read to the lodge at the installation of Rising Star on 27 June 1888:

> Bloemfontein 22 June 1888
>
> W, Sir and Brother,
>
> Ever since I became a resident of the Orange Free State it was my pleasant privilege, except in the year 1872 when I was attacked by a long and severe illness, to assist in the ceremony of installation of the Most W Master and the investiture of his officers.
>
> The recent severe illness through which by God's goodness I have so well recovered renders it necessary that I should take very great care and not go out in the evening. It is therefore with great regret that I am prevented from enjoying the privilege of being present at the installation of your Master and the investiture of his officers to which I have so kindly been invited by your note of the twenty first instant.

I am yours fraternally,
J. H. Brand

His illness had started the previous year and Leander Starr Jameson, a doctor from Kimberley, was called to treat him, but he died the following month. Maude Bidwell remembers his funeral: 'It was a sunny Sunday morning and all the bells were tolling. The Fichardt children picked violets which their mother made into a large wreath.'

Much was said at the funeral in Bloemfontein and the Lodge of Sorrows and memorial service in Cape Town, which were attended by every level of society. The following pertinent lines were delivered at his graveside by the Landdrost of Bloemfontein, Brother de Beer:

> My friends, it is not only the Volksraad and the people who have suffered a heavy loss but the Executive also loses in him a sincere friend who always consulted on important matters, gratefully acknowledged advice which he considered acceptable, and when he differed from us he never spoke as one wielding authority but invariably showed that he respected the opinions of others. Brethren was it not agreeable when he was present at our labours? Did we not rejoice at owning such a Brother? And when he was not present have we not had tangible proof of his fraternal love and sympathy?
>
> When his Honour assumed the Government of the State he at once took hammer and chisel and other implements in hand to reduce the rough block, the Orange Free State, to symmetry – for four and twenty

years, five months and twelve days he laboured, making that rough block what it is today.

The *South African Freemason* of 11 September 1888 reported:

A Lodge of Sorrows was held in Cape Town on 25 August 1888 for our late Brother, the Honourable Johannes Hendricus Brand, under the guidance of the M. Wor Bro John Fredrick Marshall. It was attended by the Governor Sir Hercules Robinson, his honour John Tudhope, the colonial secretary, Sir David Tennant, the speaker, and a large complement of Brethren. It was so well attended that entrance was by ticket only.

Two of the orations given at the Lodge of Sorrows leave us with the following on Johannes Brand. Provincial Grand Master Brother Reverend D. P. Faure said:

Freemasonry has had no inconsiderable share in educating the President. Men frequently asked contemptuously "What is the practical use of Freemasonry?" He freely admitted even then, in the presence of so many profanes [non-Masons]... it was Freemasonry which has given him to South Africa. He not only understood Freemasonry but it was his constant aim and endeavour to give practical effect to their aims. He was a promoter of peace and therefore a good Mason. Would that Freemasons (and all men) all over the world were imbued with [that] principle as Sir J. H. Brand was, then peace should reign all over the earth.

The orator Brother Daulier said:

> Love for his brethren, pleasant companionship, active promotion of every good cause, benevolence in its truest and most exalted sense, unshaken courage under trials and disappointment, thankfulness in gifts of the past and hopefulness in the future, were principal traits of his character. God fearing, deeply attached to his native land.

From the grave Brand implores us to love and serve the country in which we live. There is no question in my mind that he was the right man at the right time and I believe his Masonry had a lot to do with his preparation for the job. He was a brilliant lawyer and a courageous military leader, of course, but a year in the Master's chair taught him how to lead without power, to discipline with compassion and to exercise his will by his example only.

President
Reitz

Chapter 11
Francis William Reitz

Francis Reitz was dumbstruck when he heard that Johannes Brand was dead. He dashed round to the Residency and shouldered through the large crowd. When he got into the house he saw Sabilia surrounded by family, but she broke away to hug him. He was like a son, sometimes a difficult one, sometimes difficult to love, but she did without reserve. 'Leave everything to me,' he whispered in her ear. He sometimes rubbed people up the wrong way, but if you wanted something done he was the one to do it. Reitz was the Chief Justice and as such was the right man to arrange the state funeral. And as a senior Mason he would ensure the lodges were not left out and went to see the Masters of both lodges.

Brand and he worked well together even though they did not always agree, especially over the Afrikanerbond. The Bond was a cultural organisation founded to stem the tide of the erosion of Dutch/Afrikaans culture and it took up most of his spare time and energy establishing branches all over the country. Brand was trying to bring English and Dutch countrymen together and there was no bad blood between the English and the Boers in the Orange Free State in those days. He felt the Bond was divisive and he could see no need for the new language, Afrikaans, that the organisation was promoting. Paul Kruger in the Transvaal also saw it as an undermining influence.

Reitz, in the face of this official disapproval, became even more zealous. At the landmark Boer unity Paardekraal celebrations in Potchefstroom in the Transvaal, he paraded himself as the Orange Free State delegate and proceeded to push the Bond's aims. In spite of criticism of being arrogant and fractious he was happy with the outcome even though Brand and Kruger were furious. This undermined his standing in Bloemfontein society, which forced him to pull his horns in a bit, and his fiercely pro-Transvaal stance lost him further support. Brand was happy to be a friend of the Transvaal, but did not want to be embroiled in their fight he could see coming with England. Brand was considered too English and Reitz hated everything English, especially the 'title' they bestowed on the president, against which he had fought openly, and only with the greatest reluctance went along with in the Volksraad. He was obviously his own man.

—•—

Reitz was born into a prominent Swellendam family on 5 October 1844. They had a 6 000-acre farm, Rhenosterfontien, where he grew up with two coloured friends, Ou Koos and Platbaaitjie. His early education began with a governess at the age of nine before he was sent to Dr Drossel's boarding school in Rondebosch. At twelve he was chosen as a Queen's scholar to attend the South African College where, for the next six years, he studied English, Latin, Greek, and ancient and English history. One of his teachers was Johannes Brand, who was fond of him, and they developed a bond which remained for the rest of their lives. It was Brand who saw a particular talent in him and encouraged him to study law.

When Brand was called to the presidency of the Orange Free State, his post as professor was taken over by an equally charismatic character, Advocate Watermeyer, under whose guidance Reitz blossomed and showed himself to be a brilliant student. Watermeyer recommended he be sent to the Inner Temple in London, where in the rarefied atmosphere of the greatest legal training ground in the world he shone.

On 11 June 1867 he returned to the Cape and was admitted to the bar on 25 January 1868. He set up a practice which was mainly involved in run-of-the-mill applications and he found himself turning to his love of writing for stimulation.

He submitted work to a number of magazines and wrote verse in the local vernacular 'Afrikaans' language, which at that time was not recognised. Because of his passion for Afrikaans, Reitz has often been regarded as one the fathers of the language that would one day replace Dutch in South Africa. His love of literature led him in two directions that would affect the rest of his life. He became political correspondent of the *Argus* newspaper, which in turn led him into politics. And as an Afrikaans poet he was instrumental in founding the Afrikanerbond, a group dedicated to the establishment of Afrikaans culture. Later it evolved from a cultural organisation into a pressure group with powerful influence.

He was first lured to the Orange Free State by the discovery of diamonds and a desire to seek his fortune. He wrote to Brand asking his advice, to which he received a hesitant reply suggesting he first visit the Orange Free State to have a look around before permanently leaving Cape Town. Undaunted, he set off for the diamond fields and wrote to Brand informing him that he had come to stay for the required month before sitting the law examination. He was disappointed when he arrived in Bloemfontein to find that there was less work there than in Cape Town. After kicking his heels in Bloemfontein he returned to Pniel where he bought a claim which produced nothing in nine months; ultimately he was forced to walk back to Cape Town. When he got there it was to find the discovery of diamonds had revived prosperity. He again started his practice, which was more successful than the first time.

Although Reitz lost his initial popularity among the people, he still had a strong following and it was generally agreed that he was the only one capable of succeeding Brand, and the Volksraad confirmed him as their only nominated candidate. Not everyone was pleased and the *Friend* newspaper challenged his stand on certain issues, to which he responded as follows:

> To become the successor of the late President Brand, who as a statesman has earned for himself undying praise throughout the civilised world, is to undertake that before which any man might well hesitate. I could not do it relying solely on my own strength, although the Volksraad nominated me unconditionally and without any previous formal confession of faith, I am fully prepared to reply that it will not surprise you, Sir, that amongst the most important questions referred to by you, I should place the United South Africa in the foreground. My fervent desire is that whilst maintaining the independence of the Free State, and whilst recognising the rights of every burgher and inhabitant of our country – the United South Africa shall have become an accomplished fact.

On 7 November the *Friend* replied with the leader, 'Can it be that the Chief Justice, Mr Reitz, has made a mistake in descending from the bench into the political arena?' Then it challenged him on a number of issues: his opposition to Brand, his partisan approach in everything, and that he was antagonistic toward other parties.

He was duly elected on 18 December 1888.

Reitz's first task as president was to find a new Chief Justice. He immediately thought of his old friend, Melius de Villiers. He could clearly remember that night on 27 May 1874 when the Master of Lodge de Goede Hoop, Jan Hendrik Hofmeyr, initiated them. It was an auspicious evening with Sir Christoffel Brand in attendance, though his old professor, Johannes Brand, could not make it. The two initiates remained friends and colleagues for the rest of their lives. Melius was also an advocate and the brother of J. H. de Villiers, the Chief Justice of the Cape.

Reitz accepted Brand's call to the Free State to be his Chief Justice almost a year after he had been elected to parliament representing Beaufort West. His practice started to prosper, but this did not dilute his love of letters or politics. He wrote to Brand from Cape Town: 'I hope to be in Bloemfontien before the end of July in order to give myself ample time to get everything in order. I was married on the 24 June 1874 and I am glad to quit the ranks of bachelorhood. If all goes well we shall start from Swellendam on the 10th.'

He had married Blanka, a member of the wealthy Thesen family of Knysna, a month after the initiation. They were very happy and produced eight children. In the words of Sophie Leviseur, a close friend of both Brand and Reitz: 'Reitz brought with him his little Swedish wife; we all loved her, she was so pretty and dainty, with plaits of gorgeous golden hair. Unfortunately she died on his birthday in 1887 and he was to assume the Presidency on his own.'

When he arrived in Bloemfontien he plunged into the life of the capital with his customary enthusiasm. He became chairman of the curators of Grey College, chairman of the agricultural committee, involved himself with both lodges, established a branch of the Afrikanerbond, and even sat on the committee of the insane asylum.

——•——

After all-night celebrations in the square on 9 January 1889, the commandos assembled there in a 'kind of formation' and fired volleys of shots into the air until ten o'clock when the President-elect marched in procession to the church to take the oath. At 11:30 he delivered his address in which he said:

> In the years that follow I shall not forget that I am the successor of President Brand. My desire is not to be only his successor but as far as possible his follower... Gentlemen, the Free State is a small country and we acknowledge that it is as yet a comparatively poor and weak country but I firmly believe that it has a great future... A young country that has committed as yet no serious mistakes is in fact more fortunate than a mighty empire.

He began by tackling the thorny question of the railway to the Transvaal. Started by Brand, the line from the Cape to the Orange Free State was completed on 17 June 1889. Before the Volksraad was a memorandum containing 6 341 signatures against and only

2 984 for the railway to the Transvaal. Those opposing it felt that the country could not afford a railway that would mainly benefit Kruger. In March 1889 Reitz met Kruger in Potchefstroom and they concluded a mutual defence treaty, which Reitz could draft. He called his own congress to discuss the customs union and his proposals were accepted.

Reitz presented these propositions at the next session of the Volksraad on 6 May and ran into a torrid time. He wanted to spend the Government's surplus on bridges over the Caledon and Vaal rivers. He insisted on answering the objections without really thinking them through and did it badly. So his presidency started on a bumpy note, but he was not a man easily deterred and he fought, lobbied and argued his case until he got his way by 15 May with 29 votes to 21 against. At the end of that year he married Cornelia Maria Mulder, a headmistress of a girls' school and together they had six sons and a daughter.

Free Staters were suspicious of his goals and he was severely criticised for his *toenadering* (rapprochement) with the Transvaal, which could possibly lead his country into a war. For a man who observed that his country had not made a serious mistake, was he about to make the biggest one in their history? While brilliant and passionate, it was also becoming obvious that he was impulsive and impatient.

When Reitz arrived in Bloemfontein, Masonry was suffering a decline as men were drawn away by mines. Many of these were single men seeking their fortune while others were married and forced to leave home to build up capital to prop up their farms. Lodge Unie finally closed to reopen at Rietkiul on the diamond fields. Reitz followed Brand in his practice of visiting both lodges at least once a year at their installation meetings. The meeting of 24 June 1889, its first installation after he assumed the presidency, records him as being present. The *South African Freemason* of 2 July 1889 reported that Reitz and de Villiers were present at the meeting of Rising Star Lodge and signed on as members of Lodge Unie. When the Raadsaal was renovated he presented to the lodge on 3 August 1893 the original President's chair from the old Volksraad, a large piece with a gothic roof that is still there today.

Perhaps his visit to the lodge brought him down to earth or the bruising he had taken from his detractors led him back to the circle of his brethren. Soon after his visit to the lodge he left on a tour of the country districts on which his approach was diplomatic and charming in dealing with country folk. They loved him, he was one of their own, knowledgeable in agricultural matters, a completely different man from the one who was aggressively defensive in the Volksraad. He started to invite people home and tried to emulate Brand's style of 'open house'. But it was never the same and older people especially were missing their old president. It was clear that Reitz would have to earn the love of his people.

———•———

Before the start of his second year in office, Reitz vacationed at his holiday home in Tamboerskloof, high above Cape Town in the foothills of Lion's Neck near the Gardens with views overlooking the bay. The home was a rambling house with a stoep between two gables – more Victorian than Cape Dutch.

'Come, you kids, clean up this place,' yelled Cornelia. 'Your uncle is coming to visit.'

'Will they bring the cousins with them?'

'I don't know, but take your things out of the lounge. I can hear the carriage.'

The Schrieners arrived with a few kids tumbling out the carriage, soon to head for the beach. Denys, Reitz's eldest son, was sent off to buy salad ingredients and the Schrieners' eldest daughter went with him.

'You must all be back for supper,' ordered Cornelia, taking Suss Schreiner with her to the kitchen. The men were on the stoep with Reitz fixing drinks.

'So tell me *swaar*, how was your first year?' enquired Schriener.

'Tough,' admitted Reitz, swinging on his deckchair.

'Be careful you don't come a cropper.'

They both laughed, Schreiner and Reitz were good friends and he was not referring to his political career, but the time they were holidaying at Bishop's Glen with the Leviseurs. It was at the time that Brand agreed to accept the knighthood and Reitz was sitting on a similar chair and became so agitated that it collapsed to the amusement of everyone, including little Sophie Leviseur who wrote about it in a class project, which was widely published.

'What are you two laughing about?' asked Cornelia, putting down the tray of coffee.

'We were remembering Bishop's Glen.'

'So, big brother, you've had a rough year,' said Suss, finding space for a cake.

'No more than the Prime Minister of the Cape,' quipped Reitz.

Schreiner and Reitz liked one another even though they headed two very different states with different ideologies.

'How much does England interfere with you?' teased Reitz.

'Not too much. We work within policy. I suppose I could ask if Kruger interferes with you.'

'Don't be mad, we're an independent country. Sure we have "Boere Unity" which we're trying to cement, but we're our own people.'

'You know the majority of our people in the Cape are also Boere. Jan Brand was enamoured by Lord Carnarvon's dream of a confederation of states in southern Africa.'

'That's just another ploy by your masters to grab the whole region.'

'Stop the politics, you two,' scolded Cornelia.

'We will in a minute,' said Schreiner. 'I think we can learn a lot from our old professor's technique of planting a thought in the minds of people and slowly nurturing it until they make it their own.'

'I don't have time for that,' responded Reitz. 'I've lots of things to do and no time for games.'

------●------

The Free Staters were looking to a bright future as 1890 dawned with a flourish. Reitz had come to his senses; perhaps from his holiday or from discussions with his brother-in-law. When he got back he tackled sensible projects: a technical division for Grey College, a school, a hospital and improvements to the education system. Legislation was also introduced to control gambling. He once more proposed the railway north to the Transvaal, this time emphasising that closer ties with the Transvaal were inevitable, and cleverly left the timing and route to the Volksraad. He arranged a Council of Delegates to consider how a federation could be brought about even though the Orange Free State's ties with the Cape would make it difficult.

On 17 December, Bloemfontein was in a fluster as the first of four trains steamed into the city. On one was Cecil John Rhodes, who together with Reitz opened the Bloemfontein–Cape Town line. The country was prospering, the railways were working, the customs agreement was in place and working well, which made it a foregone conclusion that Reitz would be nominated and re-elected for a second term. He was sworn in on 10 January 1894 and the *Friend* reported that the President's speech dealt with extremely commonplace subjects. At the end it he applied for six weeks' leave to go with his family to Europe, which was granted. They were received by the Queen of the Netherlands, President Casimer Perier of France, King Leopold of Belgium, Sir Walter Scott, to whom they presented a lion skin, and Sir George Grey.

On his return he was found to be very ill. It was believed he had contracted jaundice in Europe and his speeches in parliament were read by Blignaut, the Government Secretary. J. C. de Waal went to see him while he was recuperating at Somerstrand and found a broken man sobbing that he had no friends. He was sent back to Europe for treatment, but there was little improvement and his demeanour changed from boyish exuberance to haggard lethargy. By November there was real concern for his health and on 19 November he summoned the Volksraad and asked them to nominate a successor. On 16 December he again left for Europe where German doctors diagnosed his condition as 'nervous debility' and successfully treated him. On his return he chose to live in the Transvaal rather than return to the Orange Free State and set up a practice in Pretoria.

In 1897 he was admitted as an advocate in the Transvaal and soon after was appointed Judge of the Supreme Court. On 12 May 1898, at the inauguration of Paul Kruger for his fourth term, Reitz was appointed as Secretary of State while Jan Smuts was appointed State Attorney. These two became Kruger's spokesmen, particularly with reference to the British question. Reitz remained inflexible to British demands and it was he who drafted the famous ultimatum to Great Britain, firmly believing the Boers could win. If only he had remembered the lessons his old mentor, Brand, had taught him – that the war may have been avoided. But this was not to be and the Anglo-Boer War began in October 1899.

When it was clear that the Boers could not win, Reitz was called on to play his most important role, that of winning the peace. He was tireless in advising, translating and debating the best terms for the Transvaal and on 31 May 1902 acting President Schalk Bergers signed the Treaty of Vereeniging; the very next signature was that of Reitz. The document avoided the term 'surrender' and accorded colonial status on the defeated republics, which was probably thanks to Reitz's efforts. In 1910 he was elected President of the Senate of the Union of South Africa. If this union was not quite the federation he had dreamed of so long ago, it was close and he was happy to serve. One cannot help wondering if he had been stronger and wiser whether he could have achieved his aims without bloodshed and hatred. It seems clear his patriotic fervour blinded him to see past his present into the future.

In March 1922 he was elected an honorary member of Lodge de Goede Hoop. In 1929 he retired to his holiday home and rejoined his brethren at the lodge, finally finding peace in the brotherhood he admired so much. On his 88th birthday, he was in lodge when an oil painting of Johannes Brand was presented to the lodge. He died in 1934.

Author's Note

The inspiration for these stories came from my research for papers presented in the Lyceum Lodge of Research No. 8682 English Constitution as well as encouragement from my brethren there, particularly George Kendall and Manfred Hermer. My friend, the author and raconteur Roger Webster, also nagged me unmercifully to put them to paper.

Wherever I have solid facts I have adhered to them as faithfully as possible, but have freely embroidered the stories with invented meetings, conversations and situations that I believe were possible. I have even obliquely hinted at an affair between Louis Thibault and Lady Anne Barnard, which has no historic substance other than that she worked with him on a number of projects and mentions him with fondness in her writings. I believe her portrait of him, the only one there is, has an intimacy about it.

Inevitably, there is a blurred line between fact and fiction and I thank my friends Pat Hopkins and Louis Greenberg for combing these lines for faults, though any errors are mine. The 'Transactions of the Lyceum Lodge of Research' contain my papers documented and referenced. They exclude any flights of imagination, so if you are looking for that level of information you may contact the secretary through the office of The District Grand Lodge of South Africa North English Constitution on +27 11 643 3311.